SUPERWOMAN

Hi Penny!
I wrote this
book to remind
you that you are
NoT alone.
Together we stand.
Together we do our best.
Hugs,
Marie

SUPER WOMAN

A FUNNY AND REFLECTIVE LOOK AT SINGLE MOTHERHOOD

MONA ANDREI

CYNREN

Published by Cynren Press
101 Lindenwood Drive, Suite 225
Malvern, PA 19355 USA
http://www.cynren.com/

Printed in the United States of America on acid-free paper

ISBN-13: 978-1-947976-22-1 (pbk)
ISBN-13: 978-1-947976-23-8 (ebk)

Library of Congress Control Number: 2020940208

Portions of "Of Course, This Book Wouldn't Be Complete
without a Chapter on the Lovely Task of Raising Teenagers"
were originally published in *Emerge Woman Magazine.*
Portions of "From Where You Are to Where You Want to
Be with the Three Cs" were originally published in *Womenz
Straight Talk Magazine.* Various portions of this book were
originally published in the author's column "Insights from the
Hood (PARENThood, That Is)," WestmountMag.ca, and on
the author's humor blog, Moxie-Dude.com.

Cover design by Tim Barber

CONTENTS

FIVE PRINCIPLES FOR LIVING
A KICK-ASS LIFE
AS A SINGLE MOM

1. Just for a moment today, I will smile for no apparent reason. People will think I'm crazy or that I just murdered someone, and I will stare them down until they look away. Smiling makes me feel good, and I deserve to feel good. That is my no apparent reason.

2. Just for a moment today, I will remind myself of the things that make me feel good. Like chocolate. And that rare occasion when I can escape to the bathroom and pee by myself.

3. Just for a moment today, I will raise an eyebrow at the Mount Everest of laundry lying on the bathroom floor. And then I'll walk away, because I can. I own the power. Not you, laundry. Me.

4. Just for a moment today, I will take a deep breath before yelling at the kids to stop fighting. During that breath, I will think about the bottle of wine waiting for me in the fridge. And then I'll yell at the kids.

5. Just for a moment today, I will remember who I am. A mother, yes. But more than that, I am a woman of substance. A woman with dreams and aspirations. A woman with a purpose and a mission. And then I will try to figure out what that purpose and mission are, because there's no way I was put on this earth to prove my point to a mound of laundry.

TO THOU WHO READS THIS BOOK . . .

I WAS GOING TO CALL this preface "Note from the Writer," but then I thought, *Duh*. This entire book is filled with notes from "the writer." That's me. Which leads us to the question, *Who the hell is "me"?*

Well, I'm the blogger behind *Moxie-Dude.com. Life updates gone wrong. Or right. I'm undecided.* With that said, feel free to call me Mona or Moxie—I go by both names. Just don't call me "Mom," because I get enough of that at home.

Now that we've gotten that out of the way, you're probably wondering why I wrote this book, or even more, why you should read it. That's a fair question, especially since my background is in marketing, and whenever I'm working on a copywriting project, I always try to work around the one question that everyone asks themselves: *What's in it for me?* (In this case, "me" means *you*.)

First and foremost, my goal with this book is to show you that as a single mother, you are not alone. I say this because when I was a young single mother, *alone* is how I felt much of the time. And while I'm not a therapist, a life coach, or Mother Teresa, I am an advocate for living your ideal life. Now most people don't put these two things together—being a single mom and living your ideal life—because solo parenting is damn hard. You know it. I know it. Your ex knows it. But although it's challenging, solo parenting is also one of the most rewarding experiences you'll ever achieve. I call it an achievement because at the end of the day—every day—you deserve a freaking award.

And that's not all. I have another reason for writing this book. When I was a young single mother, I would have loved for someone to tell me not to define myself by my status, to get out of survival mode and turn on the go-get-it switch. My message in this book is that for life to be a truly satisfying experience, you must live it as your authentic self. But for you to understand the power behind my message, you have to know where I've been, which is why I share so much of my personal life with you in this book.

Once upon a very long time ago, I would travel every week from my home in the suburbs of Montreal to New York City. At the time, I was following my dream to be an actress, and every week, I would take an eight-hour bus ride to study with an acting coach I admired. What I remember most about this teacher was his use of a certain expression. In fact, he used it a lot.

"Youth is wasted on the young," he would say.

I didn't take this as a deliberate reflection on me personally—even though he almost always looked at me when he said it. And although I had the deepest respect for this man when it came to acting technique, as far as I was concerned, he was 157 years old and knew nothing of the ways of contemporary life. At the time, my worldly definition of "youth" was anyone under four years old. (I'm not proud of that.)

Fast-forward to today. I'm still a few years short of being 157 years old and will probably never amass the amount of wisdom my former acting coach possessed. But I can finally boast an understanding of what this very wise man was trying to say: that *youth is wasted on the young.*

It's taken me many years (read: *wasted time*) and disappointments (read: *stupid decisions*) to get to this point in my life, when I can say—with complete honesty—that I'm happy with myself, with who I am, and with the life I've created. I can say with conviction that I'm living my ideal life. I have found my purpose. But here's the thing: my purpose has always been right here with me, except that I was too busy entertaining thoughts of distractions and self-doubt to see it.

Nowadays, it is with great pride (and hardly any feelings of insecurity) that I proclaim who and what I am. Part of who I am is a writer. I get to write every day—on my blog, on my book endeavors, on client projects. I get to connect, share, entertain, and inspire through words. Where once I thought it only a dream, I realize now that dreams *can* become a reality—*if* you believe in yourself, and *if* you persevere.

My only wish? That I hadn't wasted so many precious years on distractions. Instead of focusing on my self-doubt and insecurities, I should have been focusing on my lifelong passion for writing. Unfortunately, I can't go back in time to bop younger me upside the head, because I'm pretty sure that this would be considered abuse on some level. But what I can do is share some of my experiences and accumulated quasi-wisdom in the hope of saving you from wasting time and experiencing disappointment. This is my hope for you.

If you're anything like younger me—a single mom wishing that life had come with a how-to manual on living your ideal life and being your authentic self—this book is for you. This book is about remembering who you are, what gives you purpose and passion. And I help you do that by sharing my own experiences.

As well, I've had the opportunity to speak with other single mothers, and I share their stories in a series of interviews interspersed throughout this book. My goal is to demonstrate that there is no right or wrong way to parent and that there are as many life options as there are moms in this world. To the lovely ladies whom I've gotten to know while writing this book, a sincere thank-you. Thank you for your time. Thank you for sharing your stories. Thank you for giving us a glimpse into your lives and the lessons you've learned.

Question: What are we without purpose and passion?
Answer: Empty.

So, who am I? I'm just a single mom who had a dream. And if what I recount in this book resonates with you, prevents you from thinking *this is it* by reminding you of *your* dreams, or perhaps gives you the confidence to stand by some of the decisions you've made, then my work is done. I'm a happy camper. (Just kidding. I hate camping.)

ONE

BREAKUPS—IN MANY WAYS, THEY'RE LIKE A BARSTOOL

MOVING, STARTING A NEW JOB, realizing that you've just burned dinner and have no backup plan—these are some of the most stressful situations in a person's life. And then there's the *breakup,* which sits in its very own corner of a dark room. No matter who initiates a breakup or the reasons for it, here's the thing: even for the right reasons, breakups are difficult. And when you have children, they're even harder, because this is when you realize that fairy tales that end with "and they lived happily ever after" are full of shit. Not because happy endings don't exist, but because for single mothers, the end of a crappy relationship is really the beginning. And it can be a beautiful beginning—*if* you allow yourself to flourish.

While a breakup may feel like the end of everything, including your life, it's actually not. Yes, it's the end of your life as you know it. But be optimistic. The end of crap can only mean that you're giving room to something better. A new beginning. That said, before you get to that promised beginning, you must prevail through four phases before you're out of the woods. Like the four legs of a barstool, these four phases are important, because going through them—and

perhaps even embracing them—will give you the foundation for moving forward on solid ground. You see, when
you're a single mother, the End is really the Beginning—the
beginning of you.

Let's walk through the phases of a breakup. My hope
here is that by becoming aware of these four phases, you'll
be able to recognize where you are and even let some of the
pain escape into the ether of "not my problem anymore."

PHASE 1. WHEN YOU REALIZE THAT YOU'VE BEEN OVERLOOKING YOURSELF

Right or wrong for each other, there's something sentimental about growing a relationship. And as a woman, I think
you'll relate when I say that we have this tendency to want
to accommodate every aspect of our lives, including the
lives of those around us—especially the men in our lives.
Accommodate, in this context, means often putting ourselves
aside so that we can focus on pleasing others. Can I get an
"amen" to that?

Then you wake up one morning and realize that you don't
even like your eggs scrambled, or war movies, or whatever
it is that you've tried or pretended to like for his sake. This
is a very scary phase, because it's time to reevaluate what
you've deemed the most important aspect of your life: your
partner. The questions that haunt you during this phase go
something like this:

What if it's me?
Am I being selfish?
What if there's no one out there for me?
What if I'm just afraid of being alone?
Am I settling?

And even though the gods-that-be do not descend and
bestow you with the answers, you wonder if maybe just
the fact that you're asking these questions is a sign. Then
something happens that pushes you to the darker side of

second-guessing yourself, and you begin to question your relationship. Is it healthy? Is it dysfunctional? The very fact that you're asking these questions makes you realize that the answers are, respectively, no and yes.

Is it healthy? *No.*

Is it dysfunctional? *Yes.*

Breaking up is never easy. If it were, there wouldn't be a gazillion songs written about it. And given that we're part of the new millennium and can say things out loud without the fear of being tied to a bed for an exorcism, I'll be the first to say it: "for better or for worse" are the five stupidest words ever to have been strung together. All this to say that, no, it's not you. If you're in a crappy relationship, get the hell out. I know it's not easy. It's damn hard. But if you're not happy with him, at least give yourself the chance to be happy without him. Take the step, and here's what happens next.

PHASE 2. WHEN YOU WAKE UP THAT FIRST MORNING AS A SINGLE MOTHER AND YOU REALIZE THAT YOU DID NOT IN FACT WAKE UP DEAD, AS YOU THOUGHT YOU WOULD

Phase 2 is probably the shortest phase of all. You ended the relationship, and not only did you survive the first night as a single person but you feel kind of good about it. You lie in bed longer than usual, because the ceiling seems to be inspiring you to make plans for your new life.

Your first plan of action is to get rid of all the evidence. Clothes in the closet, man things in the bathroom, left-behind beer in the fridge—all must go. And suddenly you realize just how much of your universe—space and time—was being sucked up by discontent and disappointment.

The hardest part of breaking up is the actual breaking up part. You realize this the moment that weight has been lifted from your shoulders. And now that he's gone, you feel liberated. You wonder why it took you so long. And guess what?

Your future—the future of your kids—stands a chance now. A chance for what? A chance to be happy. A chance to try new things. A chance to discover who you really are without the burden of unhappiness. Let's face it. Unhappiness is a distraction. You're now free. Perhaps even freer than you've ever been in your life. Whoa! That. Is. HUGE.

PHASE 3. WHEN YOU SET UP CAMP BESIDE THE HAMSTER

Phase 3 is the saddest part of a breakup. It's also the most volatile. Just like the unsteadiness of a three-legged barstool, you have to be very careful as to where you place your weight. And by *weight,* I mean *focus.* This is when you go inward. Suddenly you realize that driving alone in your car has turned into a sweat lodge for your emotions. The lyrics to every song on the radio hijack your memories—all the shared dreams and conversations—and it dawns on you that, oh my goodness, maybe you made a mistake!

What if it *was* me?

What if I *was* being selfish?

What if he really *was* the one?

What if I *wasn't* settling?

And so, you call your mom and tell her what the hamster is now trying to make you believe—that you *have* to call him back. And your mom confirms what your now-ex has been trying to tell you in the gazillion texts and voicemails he's been sending you since the breakup: he's not a bad person; he just made some mistakes.

And then you think, *One mistake . . . two mistakes*—but after *years* of mistakes, the word *mistake* defined the entire relationship.

Phase 3 is the saddest, the longest, and the most unstable of all the breakup phases. The key is not to let yourself think about the good things but to remind yourself of the parts that should have been classified as "unacceptable." You know what I'm talking about. Perhaps you have the bruises to show for it. Perhaps those bruises weren't on your body but on your spirit and emotions. Did he support you in your dreams and aspirations? No, he belittled you? That's abuse.

Phase 3 is a little like a detox diet. You have to keep *you* in mind until you get him out of your system. And then one day . . .

PHASE 4. WHEN YOU WAKE UP ONE NEW MORNING, TAKE A DEEP BREATH, AND REALIZE THAT YOU'VE SET YOURSELF UP WITH A BARSTOOL COMPLETE WITH FOUR LEGS—AND STRONG ENOUGH FOR YOU TO SIT ON BY YOURSELF

This is the day that you notice the sun has melted a thin layer of the sadness that grew around both your perception and your awareness. It's also the day that you choose to keep many of the pieces from that relationship in your heart, because perhaps he really isn't a bad person. There were times when you really did believe that love meant forever, no matter what. You're just realizing now that forever wasn't meant to be with him.

There's a saying that people come into our lives either for a reason, a season, or a lifetime. The reason is easy to understand. Teachers come in many forms, and we really can learn from everyone. A lifetime—well, isn't that the goal? To have someone to love, admire, and respect, someone you can count on until death really does you part? Not as easy to understand is the "season." I struggled with this for a long time. Why do people come into our lives if it's not for a reason or a lifetime? And then it dawned on me—sometimes *we* are the reason to cross another's path. Sometimes *we* have something to offer or a lesson to share.

Regardless, when it comes time to letting go of someone— even if he's the father of your children—moving on can be the greatest gift that you give yourself, even if it means leaving a piece of yourself behind. You may feel sentimental, because leaving a piece of yourself behind is never easy. But once you realize that that piece is simply no longer serving you, moving on becomes easier.

When I first became a single mother, and even over the days and weeks leading up to it, I went through all the phases. The questioning. The sadness. The melancholy. Even the regrets. I've said this before: becoming a single mother was not what I had imagined for myself. And I do remember how difficult it was to finally accept the fact that I had chosen the wrong men to have children with. While I'm still friends to this day with the father of my two youngest children, I'm the first to admit that all I ever wanted was a family. And in my "want," I didn't take the time to vet what a family meant to me. Perhaps self-doubt and even issues with self-esteem played a part in my choices of what paths to take. I take full responsibility for this. And the journey continued even after the breakups. I went from feeling alone and thinking that life hated me to realizing that I was not my status and that I had something to offer the world. It all comes down to letting yourself flourish as you live through the struggles and realize just how powerful you are.

There's strength, and then there's power. As a single mom, strength is a given. We do it all, no matter how exhausted we are at the end of the day. And the following morning, we get up and do it all over again. Alone. That right there is strength, and don't you ever doubt yourself.

As for the power, you've got that too. You have the right to live your life on your terms and with a sense of meaning. It's all about finding your purpose, because living without a sense of purpose is like eating Kraft dinner—it fills the void, but there's no oomph.

TWO

A MOTHER'S SIXTH SENSE— THAT DAMN SENSE OF GUILT

HAVE YOU NOTICED THAT SINCE becoming a parent, you've developed an uncanny sense of guilt? Oh, sure. It was there *before* you had kids and would occasionally come out of hiding. Like when someone asked you what you did the previous night, and you answered, "Not much," when really "not much" translates into binge-watching *Tiger King* on Netflix while devouring an entire box of Triscuits. (Or maybe that's just me.) But *that* guilt is nothing compared to the sense of guilt that wakes up inside of you soon after you've given birth.

What is guilt anyway? An emotion? A living, thriving part of your personality? A cousin to shame? The mother of regret? Hard to define, yet forcefully present in its evasiveness, guilt has a way of eating at your brain and chewing on your soul. We're all born with a sense of guilt (except maybe narcissists and serial killers), yet it seems almost dormant until you become a caregiver to little humans.

Scenario: You've accepted a newly invented position in the world of pretend jobs, and your title is Chief Word Herder. It's your first day, and you're getting settled at your new desk next to a window overlooking a park. *Not bad,* you think to yourself. *Chief Word Herder* and *a view. How hard can this be?* All is well and good, until you realize that the park makes you think of your kids. (Guilt can be subtle.)

"Focus," you tell yourself. A job is a good thing, because it means paid bills and food and new shoes for the kids every six months. (When you become a mother, it suddenly doesn't matter that you've been wearing the same underwear since 2007. But your kids? Different story.) As you're having this conversation with guilt, your new boss walks up to your desk with your first assignment.

"Find a flavor that relates to the word *guilt*," she asks of you.

Hmm . . . give guilt a flavor, you think. *Coincidence?* You open a new Word document on your computer and start listing whatever pops into your head: sweet, sour, spicy, chicken wings, spaghetti . . . Suddenly your mind stops in its tracks as it comes face-to-face with an avalanche of memories.

The morning you dropped your daughter off at day care *knowing* she was coming down with a cold, but you felt you had no choice because you'd taken a day off when your son was sick just last week.

The time you yelled at your son for no other reason than your own tired frustration while he took forever to put on his shoes.

The evening you resented your kids for having *so much homework.*

That's when it hits you: you know exactly what guilt tastes like. It's a cutting mixture of sour milk and dandelions. You swallow and realize that the flavor sticks to the back of your throat like tomato paste mixed with peanut butter. You wonder if "heavy heart" is a food group.

Something happens when you become a mother. That quasi-dormant sixth sense wakes up like a fire drill going off in the middle of the night. Resonating from deep inside your chest, it's impossible to ignore. Oh, you may "know" when your kids need you (even when they're in another room), but I'm not talking about a mother's intuition. Nope. I'm talking about that nagging sixth sense that settles deep within your core and wraps itself around your juicy heart like a boa constrictor around its unwary prey. I'm talking about a mother's sense of *guilt*. Ironically, this sixth sense is usually paired with words that rhyme with *motherhood*—words like *could, should,* and *would.*

It's Friday night. I *could* let the kids stay up an extra half hour—but it's been a long week, and I just want to go to bed with a book.

I *should* make a proper meal tonight—but it's already late, and besides, doesn't frozen pizza have all the food groups?

I *would* have sent the kids to school wearing their Halloween costumes this morning—but apparently I forgot to read the damn newsletter from the school last week.

Admittedly, we all want the best for our kids. As single mothers, we're raising them alone yet strive to provide a family atmosphere. And I'm certain you'll agree when I say that we try. Oh, how we try. But let's be honest with ourselves: when we're wearing all the things (the pants, the skirt, and the world wrapped around our shoulders like a heavy shawl on a hot summer day), life becomes a juggling game. And OMG, all the things—*they just never stop.*

Alone, you manage everything, from the budget (*pfft,* what budget?) to household chores, the job, and everything going on inside your head. You even manage your emotions—the happiness, the sadness, the bewilderment, the fear, the sense of aloneness. You may not be lonely, but you *are* alone. And by yourself, you keep all in check with a constant stream of self-reminders to be patient, to take a breath before you react. (Some days you can boast the patience of Gandhi; other days you're more like the Incredible Hulk, throwing a tantrum at the slightest resistance from your kids after the seventh time you've told them to brush their teeth.) Deep down, you know that the "family unit" is only as strong as you are. Some days you're the pillar, sturdy and resilient—it takes a special kind of strength to make light of the milk that gets spilled across the table at the end of a long day. "It's okay," you say as you jump up to get the dishcloth. "It was an accident." Other days your inner pillar of strength is reduced to the size of a fire hydrant that gets peed on by every dog in the neighborhood. Sometimes it even feels like Life Herself is peeing on you every chance she gets. (The bitch.)

That glass of milk that just got spilled across the table *(again)*? It's not okay. Nope. *Not today*! It's been a long one, and I'm tired. I do not have the patience for this. Oops. And there it is. The guilt.

Several years ago, a friend (single and without children at the time) took it upon himself to impart his limited knowledge of parenting to me. "All mothers feel guilty," he'd said. He was trying to make me feel better.

To give you context, it was a Wednesday evening, and I was sitting, feeling deflated, in a classroom. Just a few hours earlier, I had left my day job at precisely 5:00 P.M. to pick up my daughters from day care, bring them home to feed them supper, and rush them out again to the babysitter's apartment. And when I say "babysitter," I mean my girls' father. (I could say "but that's another story," but as we all know, it's part of the same story, isn't it?)

My friend with all the wisdom—I knew his intentions were good. Regardless, his words cast a dark shadow of self-reproach around the muddled blur of the day that sat heavy on my slouching shoulders. To be perfectly honest, I felt like a neon light was flashing across my forehead like the signs that glow above the doorways to Chinese restaurants. Only instead of promoting dumplings in peanut sauce, my sign was screaming "World's Worst Mother" in bold, red letters.

I remember life back then as a constant, harried struggle. Monday to Friday, my girls and I would leave our apartment at 6:15 every morning and walk to the bus stop. Our mission was to get to the day care for seven o'clock, as soon as it opened, so that I could catch the next bus, which would take me to downtown Montreal. The goal: to be at my desk by eight.

Confession: I was often late. And by often, I mean *always*. Before I continue, I need to take a moment to appreciate my boss at the time. We'll call him Mr. P.

Mr. P. pretended never to notice me walking (mostly running) into the office, usually around 8:20. How do I know that he was pretending not to notice? One morning I walked into the office a few minutes *before* eight (the gods of matching socks and traffic were kind to us that day); he saw me, looked down at his watch, and, with an exaggerated "I'm your boss" voice, said, "Mona, you're early. You're fired."

Then he smiled and winked. I remember laughing, but it was more from a sense of relief than amusement. You see, every morning was a race against time, and I truly did my best to respect office hours. But there was always *something*: my sleepyhead daughters taking their sweet time to eat their toast, getting halfway down the street to the bus stop and suddenly realizing that I'd forgotten a lunch. Yet clearly, my boss, in his quiet way, looked past my daily madness of getting my ass to work on time and focused on my abilities. Although we never spoke about it, from that moment on, I felt that he was silently cheering me on. He gave me the encouragement I needed. He let me know with his subtle understanding that he somehow understood my life.

As for my friend, the one with the good intentions—the one who told me that all mothers feel guilty—I have to agree with him. All mothers, whether single, married, divorced, step, or foster, live with guilt.

Well, here's the thing: *guilt is a lie.*

Let's go back to the day you gave birth . . .

Think about the first time you looked into your new baby's tender, old-man face. (Oh, come on! Newborns are rarely as cute as we pretend they are.) After hours of heavy pushing and pain and temporary insanity, the rest of the world slipped away, and it was just you, lying in the eye of the hurricane, holding the sweetness that you had been carrying for the last nine months (which felt like nine years). The moment brought tears to your soul, didn't it?

Meanwhile, the doctors and nurses, everyone else in the room, watched in awe as mommy and new baby bonded in natural, naked glory. Legs still in stirrups yet long forgotten, hair sticking to the sides of your sweaty face, emotions hijacking your heart and soul, you were completely oblivious to the indecency of your dignity. For the doctors and nurses, it was just another day on the job. No need to cringe in shame, because once the task of assisting with childbirth is accomplished, the last thing anyone is focusing on are your exposed and mangled private parts. But you know this already. From their perspective, their job of helping to deliver your new baby is done. Now what they get to witness is an emotional moment, a phenomenon of beautiful proportions—a mother's love reduced to its purest and unaltered state during the first moments of her child's life.

But you and me, we've been on this side of the stirrups, and we know what's really going on. Those tears of joy that spill out through exhausted eye sockets are actually tears of terror. As you look down into that tiny face, so new and so trusting, you're crying because your greatest wish is that time would freeze. You're not asking for much. Just a few years. This is because in that moment in time, innocence is still shiny new with slimy, untampered perfection. You have not yet screwed up.

You know that perfection can't last forever. At some point, exhaustion, frustration, *life,* will butt in, and you'll react in a way that puts a corroded dent in the perspective you have of yourself as a mother. But for these few seconds, right after giving birth, everything is still flawless. The innocence and trust of your child have not yet been wrecked by the struggles of daily challenges and overtiredness and disappointment in how things actually turned out. The funny thing about being a mother in general, and a single mother in particular, is that you believe that this sixth sense—this sense of guilt—is unique to you. That only *you* make wrong decisions and choices. That only *you* react in ways that make you look like a raving lunatic.

You imagine that guilt is kinder to "real" families—the ones with both a mommy and a daddy. This is because real families are built on four legs, not just your volatile pillar of fake strength, but on *four* legs—mommy's legs + daddy's legs. And as everyone knows, four legs are always better than two. Four legs are so much sturdier, as proven by tables, chairs, and bar stools. It's so much easier to carry the responsibility of your children's welfare when you have someone to share it with. Or so I've heard.

Myth: Every other single mother on the planet is doing a better job than you at raising normal, happy children.

Truth: Every single mother in the world believes that she is—on most days—the worst mother on the planet. Always tired. Always rushing. Always worrying. Our aptitude for motherhood, single or not, isn't the problem. The problem is our capacity to pour a thick, syrupy layer of self-doubt over everything we do.

Repeat after me: *Guilt is a lie.*

When it comes to our kids, we all have bragging rights. They do something awesome; we tell our friends and colleagues about it. But do we tell the whole story? Most often not.

What we say: My daughter got an A on her science project.

The tiny detail we neglect to mention: After putting her to bed, I stayed up until two o'clock in the morning to finish gluing all the tiny pieces together.

What we say: My son made supper last night. I don't know where he's learning to cook—certainly not from me. I'm starting to think he's adopted.

The tiny detail we neglect to mention: I spent the rest of the evening cleaning up the kitchen, including emptying the entire fridge to clean up the juice that got spilled.

What we say: The baby is almost sleeping through the night.
The tiny detail we neglect to mention: Thank GAWD! Because I've been taking on freelance projects at night just to make ends meet.

You see where I'm going with this, don't you? We often get so wrapped up in our own sense of guilt that we forget to mention the good stuff we do—the parts of us we share unconditionally. And we do this despite the fact that there is no immediate return on our investment of time and self. Well, except maybe a tender "good night, Mommy" and a tight hug from little arms as we tuck in the day. This is what makes everything worth it. Always. And while it's true that we will screw up, I can tell you from experience that in the end, whether it be the end of a long day or after the kids have grown up, the good stuff is what we'll remember the most. The memories, the time spent, the kind words of encouragement. This is what sticks.

Don't focus on the guilt. It never tells the truth, and it feeds off of your attention. By feeling it, you give it power. Instead, focus on those tiny smiles and wide grins. Your child's happiness also feeds off your attention. So, give guilt what it deserves (a boot in the ass), and give that attention to your child, knowing that everything always works out.

Thoughts on a successful divorce

SHOW ME A SINGLE MOTHER—BY choice or circumstance—and I'll show you a woman who looks in the mirror and, on most mornings, is greeted by a reflection of her own self-doubt. I can't explain why, but something happens when we become caregivers to little human beings that we call our very own. We become self-critical. Although our hearts overflow with a desire to give and provide only the very best, our very best suddenly isn't good enough.

Sometimes the guilt stems from the very foundation of our life situation: our status as single parents. We work double-duty to provide a happy home for our kids. We know that balance is key to a healthy environment. And yet how can we possibly provide a balanced, healthy environment in a household that stands on the pillars of our two single legs?

We look at others in situations of difficulty or hardship, and our eyes glean an unspoken compassion. Yet our empathy seems to flow in a single direction: outward. And never toward ourselves.

Although no one can deny that the single mother is strong and brave, it takes a certain kind of strength and courage to accept our very best for what it is. When it comes to coping, managing, and self-acceptance, we all have our stories.

Wendy describes her early years of parenting as the "quintessential family of four": two parents, two daughters. And blessed they were indeed, because doctors had told Wendy that she would never have children owing to a thyroid disease that later evolved into a cancer diagnosis. At the time, Wendy was twenty-four years old.

Then one day, after some blood work, she received a call. To her surprise, she was pregnant. Her doctors believed that the cancer treatments had spiked an ovulation, causing her to conceive.

"This was a big miracle for me and so unexpected," Wendy recalls.

The call came while she was at work, and for the rest of the day, as you can imagine, Wendy's challenge was to stifle her excitement and to keep her news a secret. Naturally, she wanted her husband to be the first to know.

Finally, the workday ended; she went home to the apartment she shared with her husband—and there she waited. And waited. Not sure how she would tell him the news, she finally opted for writing a special note, which she gently folded and placed in a jewelry box.

Exhausted from his day at work, her husband finally walked through the door and immediately lay on the couch. For him, it was just another day, but only for a few moments more. Wendy, unable to contain her excitement any longer, scooched alongside her husband on the couch and handed him the tiny, gift-wrapped box.

"I know it's not Christmas yet." The look on his face was one of suspicion. Described as not a very expressive man, even stoic at times, her husband's face revealed a reluctance to accept the gift.

"I think he felt guilty that he didn't have something for me," Wendy recalls. "And we didn't have much money back then, so I'm sure that the little wrapped box worried him. But I told him, 'Just open it, and you'll understand.'"

Slowly, and with an obvious sense of appeasement, he unwrapped the box and pulled out the folded piece of paper.

"Guess who's going to be a daddy? You are. Ha ha! I'm pregnant," the note read.

Wendy's intention to surprise her husband with the news as a gift was a success.

"It took a few minutes for the words to register, but I'll never forget . . . it took his breath away," she says as she looks down at her hands in an attempt to hide the smile that this distant memory has evoked.

Throughout their nine years together, Wendy had never seen her husband react in this way. He was overcome with emotion. Three years later, Wendy and her husband were blessed with another miracle when they conceived their second daughter.

Though the marriage eventually led to a very difficult and hurtful breakup, Wendy stands by her conviction that how it ended is not how it was in the beginning—a sentiment she reinforces openly with her daughters.

"I think it's very important to always keep in mind the journey you had when you made that child with somebody. And even though you're not together anymore, and you're a single mom, you have to keep it in perspective," Wendy explains. "I've always told my girls that even though their father and I are no longer together, they really were made with love. We really, really wanted children."

To Wendy's point, no matter how bitter or disappointing a relationship becomes, at one time, you were on the same team.

"As single mothers, life becomes both different and difficult because we push on and we try to be strong and we try to be independent. And we have to be. We're not given a choice. And to relive the happier times can be very painful. But I think that you do a disservice to your children if you don't relive the good memories for your children's sake."

In speaking with Wendy, I discovered her respect for a specific term: *successful divorce*.

While this may seem an oxymoron and in direct opposition to the realities of a failed marriage, for Wendy, any separated couple that is able to share their children's agendas and schedules, or communicate and even be friends with the ability to move on and continue to coparent, is living a successful divorce.

Sadly, the twenty-five-year relationship between Wendy and her husband eventually reached a point where they needed to end the marriage. During the bitter divorce battle, many unwelcomed truths surfaced. Regardless, Wendy's goal throughout was to ensure that her daughters didn't suffer over the course of the proceedings.

"My biggest challenge during the divorce was in trying to make sure that my kids got through it in the healthiest way possible," recalls Wendy. "And in my guilt, I later found out that I was doing everything wrong. I was advocating for my ex-husband as I'd always done. I'd tell my kids, 'Go tell Daddy what you got on your test.' Or constantly reminding them that 'Daddy loves you.' I even made excuses for him every time he was late to pick them up. I remember the social worker telling me to stop doing that. It was really the best advice I ever received. I was lying to my children on his behalf, and it was the wrong thing to do."

Ironically, it was during the same time of year as when Wendy and her husband initially learned that they were going to have their first daughter that the couple met with a social worker to find out the best way to separate for the kids' sake. They were told not to do it during the holiday season, because then their daughters would always associate Christmas with the divorce.

"So we decided to wait until after the holidays. Meanwhile,

we continued to be as civil as possible to each other," recalls Wendy.

After the holidays, Wendy and her husband went forward with the divorce procedures, and it was at this time that she realized just how uninvolved her husband was with their children, even during their marriage.

"While filling out forms, he kept asking me questions, like what school they went to, what years they were born in—he even couldn't remember how to spell one of our daughter's middle names," Wendy recalls.

Sadly, the girls also felt their father's detachment. And although they tried to keep their unhappiness to themselves, their behavior told a different story. Every second weekend, when they had to visit with their father, who by now had moved in with his mother, the girls were miserable. They didn't want to go.

Although not apparent during their marriage, since Wendy was a stay-at-home mom whose main functions included taking care of the children and household, her husband's inert bond toward their children became clear during their separation and divorce journey.

Eventually, the girls made a unanimous decision that would impact everyone. They chose to stop all contact with their father. In her heart of hearts, Wendy knows that she did everything possible to make her daughters understand that their decision was not a frivolous one. And that it came with responsibilities.

For example, she remembers one year in particular when they received a Christmas card from their father.

"I asked my girls if they wanted to open it, and at first, they said yes. But then I explained to them that they couldn't accept things without giving back. And I told them that if they opened the card, they would have to call their father to thank him.

"I wanted my kids to learn the impact that their decisions have and that they couldn't be hypocritical."

The last time the girls spoke to their father was in 2008. When asked if she feels any guilt, Wendy's response is one of conviction.

"Do I have guilt for that? Not anymore."

Although sad and disappointing for all involved, Wendy's story demonstrates that being a parent comes with some hard-learned choices and decisions. But if you remain committed to your cause—in Wendy's case, it was to protect her children from further hurt and damage—then you can't have regret. "And if you don't have regret, you can't carry guilt." Wise words from a superwoman.

THREE

SOME THINGS GET BETTER WITH AGE, INCLUDING THE WAY WE SEE THINGS

As PARENTS IN GENERAL, AND single mothers in particular, it's important for our own sanity that we never, *ever* use the words *perfect* and *parenting* in the same sentence. We really are our own worst enemies, and this stems from a superhuman ability to look at ourselves from the outside and judge our every thought, our every decision, our every reaction. In truth, a *little* guilt is a good sign. It means we care about our children. It means we really want the best for them. And even though our envisioned best may not meet with expectations of fairy-tale lives, our best *is* the best. Truly.

I thought long and hard about whether I should share the following story, because the memory of it is tangled in the barbed wire fence that separates Desperate from Ridiculous. With no support from my girls' father on any level, including financial and parental, I think back to the days when my relationship with feelings of desperation felt like a familiar yet unwanted friend. You know that the association is "bad" for you, yet you cling to it, because there seems to be no other option. Ridiculous, on the other hand, shows to what lengths we'll go to make everything okay, and even appear normal. I hesitate to use the word *normal,* because throughout the years, I've learned that "normal" is not about what we think it is. It's more about expectations—usually, the expectations of others or the expectations of the voices inside our own heads. As I've come to learn, normal is whatever you want it to be. Normal is your own traditions and routines, regardless of your circumstances.

Remembering the extent to which I went to find things to do with my kids—activities that didn't cost money because I lived from paycheck to paycheck—makes me wonder if I didn't suffer from borderline *absurdisitis.* (Not a diagnosed condition, but if you've ever traveled down this path, you know what I'm talking about.)

After speaking with my eldest daughter, now in her thirties, and getting her perspective, I realized that while I recall the following with a tinge of shame and a dash of absurdity, my daughter remembers it with a sense of fairy-dust magic. Who knew? And so it is with my daughter's encouragement that I share this memory.

When my girls were young—six and three years old at the time—we lived in a third-floor apartment on the less-than-affluent side of town. With more concrete than grass, our neighborhood was littered with red-bricked apartment buildings on busy streets that never slept. The sound of cars speeding, angry horns, and screeching tires was the twenty-four-hour scenery for our ears. I wanted nothing more than to give my kids magical days at the amusement park or take them to the latest Disney movie, and I was very good at discrediting myself for not having the money to do any of these things.

Taking the bus to a park in greener neighborhoods or going for walks on sunny Saturdays was a given. But some weekends (and by some, I mean many), we endured days of weather-induced imprisonment, rainy days that hijacked our freedom and kept us indoors. Holding two young children hostage in an apartment for an entire weekend sounds easy now that the iPad and video games have been invented, but back then, it was a challenge—a cruel challenge to both young children and their parents.

This particular memory takes place on a Sunday morning, and it started with my girls fighting out of boredom soon after breakfast. What to do, what to do? In an attempt to distract them, I told them to get dressed because I had a surprise for them. The arguing stopped, replaced by the pitter-patter of tiny feet running toward their shared bedroom. Boredom had just been replaced by excitement and expectations.

"A *surprise*? What is it?" they asked as I snapped up their matching pink raincoats.

"Ah. It's a secret," I said. "If I tell you, it won't be a surprise." To be honest, this surprise was a secret even to me. Equipped with umbrella and anticipation, what I remember most about our walk to the bus stop were the dimples on my girls' faces. "Come *on*, Mommy." We just couldn't get to the bus stop fast enough.

They were quiet on the bus. I knew that their imaginations were conjuring up visions of grandness. A pony ride? A rare and special trip to the toy store? *What could it be*? Every once in a while, their beaming faces would look up at mine. Without words, I would encourage them to be patient. Somehow, I'd learned to make my eyes twinkle. I was in possession of a secret, and it was a special secret just for them. To this day, I believe I deserved an Academy Award for that one. But what was I really thinking?

"Where the hell am I going to take them that's fun and, most importantly, *free*?"

I only had enough money for our return bus fare, and although the rain had subsided, it was still a gray and wet day. Not the ideal day for practicing cartwheels at the park. We were headed in the direction of downtown Montreal. I remember looking out the bus window and noticing the distant dome of Saint Joseph's Oratory peeking proudly out of the city's mountain. That's when it dawned on me that entry into this majestic and historic temple may be, well, free. *And* could even feel like a visit to a magical castle. Maybe. Perhaps. I was hopeful.

As we got off the bus and started walking toward my conjured plan for a "surprise" that wouldn't disappoint, the girls begged for me to tell them where we were going. The funny thing about kids is that although they love surprises, the anticipation is torture for them. (Yes, that was my sense of *guilt* talking.) And so, to amuse them, I began to tell them a story about a castle. The tale unfolded one sentence at a time, even to myself.

While I managed to invent a story that captured their attention, part of me (actually, most of me) worried that our destination would not meet their expectations. I could only be optimistic. From afar (and by afar, I mean a stunted walking distance for tiny legs), the "castle" was enough to widen both smiles and eyes. It was majestic. It was mysterious. And as they listened to my story, their young yet clever minds suddenly put two and two together, and they screamed, "That's the castle from the story, Mommy!" We climbed the many steps to its magical magnificence until finally we were inside. At first the girls were intrigued. Craning their necks like curious goslings, they seemed to be looking for something. Something to do or to play with, I realized. It wasn't long before the intimidation of an imposed silence switched into boredom. They didn't speak it, but I could see it on their faces. The magic had disappeared, and so had their dimples.

Driven by the dread that I had disappointed them, I brought my girls outside, where we could talk freely without a few stern looks from the more serious visitors. Looking around at the grounds and building's architecture, I suddenly realized that all the nooks and crannies outside had more potential than would meet the average eye. This is when the idea hit me. Taking a wide-legged stance (something I may have picked up from an old Three Musketeers movie), and in my most animated-badass-superhero voice, I said, "Take out your swords, girls!" And with an exaggerated arm movement, I removed an invisible sword from an invisible sheath. "We have dragons to slay!"

Anyone looking would have seen a young mother and her two daughters jumping puddles in the rain and poking the air with lengthy arms. But what we saw was something extraordinary! We were dodging breaths of fire aimed at us from swooping dragons and taking cover under arched passageways made of medieval stone (in our imaginations, of course). Our mission? To save the castle from the dangers of an attack by evil creatures, unseen to the average eye. The rain? Oh. That's what gave us our superhero powers. We were soaking wet, but we were mighty.

During the bus ride home, water dripped from our faces and hair, but we didn't care. We were soaked and giggly. There's just something about saving the world that makes you feel good about yourself. And while our job as guardians of the castle was really just an entertaining way to pass a rainy Sunday afternoon, by the time I put the girls and their happy little faces to bed that night, I really did feel like I had saved the day. Remembering this piece of time, when my girls were so young and still mine, makes me realize that while I was busy letting guilt consume me, something special was also being created: memories. And the best ones, I realize now, didn't even cost a penny.

Today I can say that walking through this maze of memories that hang like well-patched comforters across a clothesline can invoke such an array of emotions. The perspective has changed, and so have the meanings. Clearly, I spent much of my time as a young, single mother hanging out with the enemy, also known as guilt. My advice to you: *don't do it*. Guilt is not your friend. And as I mentioned earlier, guilt lies! The truth is that it's okay to be tired. It's okay to vent. It's even okay to feel frustrated. If the windows are open and the neighbors hear you yelling, this doesn't make you a bad mother. It makes you human. (And who cares what the neighbors think anyway, right?)

Yes, we will screw up. We'll yell when we shouldn't. We'll blame our kids for the amount of homework they have. We'll even resent Martha Stewart for our lack of homemaking skills. The good news is that kids are resilient. And while they may believe that we're perfect, our screwups are an opportunity, a chance to show our children that it's okay to be wrong sometimes. It's okay to be so tired that you let tomorrow take care of the dishes or vacuuming. Dust bunnies that roll out from under the couch when a friend drops in—this doesn't define us but rather reveals that our limited time has been spent elsewhere. Why make a big deal out of nothing? And besides, if that friend is really your friend, she'll care more about whether you have a bottle of wine in the fridge than the dust.

A CHAT WITH
NANCY VONK
ONTARIO, CANADA

Thoughts on Juggling parenting and a career

THE YEAR 1998 WAS A big one for Nancy. On the career side of her life, she had just been promoted to co-chief creative officer for Ogilvy and Mather, an award-winning marketing agency. At home, things were a little different. She was getting divorced from her husband of nine years. She was stepping into a top creative position and, at the same time, the role of single mother.

"Becoming a single mother to my daughter, who was five years old at the time, and having a big job was not easy for either of us," Nancy says as she thinks back on the experience of juggling both a career and solo parenting.

Regardless of her title at a top Canadian agency, Nancy always felt that being a mom was her primary and most important job. She made it her priority to take her daughter to school every morning. She made sure to be home for dinner every night. She didn't go on as many business trips as she probably should have, and when she did go away, she never lingered longer than she had to for the sake of getting back to her daughter as quickly as possible. And yet, with all these boundaries, Nancy still wears a fringe of regret.

"I truly wish I had a shitload of do-overs," Nancy admits with candor. And to her point, I don't know a single parent who doesn't wish for the same opportunity. As hard as we try to do right by our children, in hindsight, and as we grow older and wiser, we come to realize that although we gave our best at the time, we could always have done something differently, made a better decision. If only we had been more aware.

"I adored my child, and yet at the time I really wasn't self-aware of what it meant to be looking at a screen so frequently while at home."

Today, Nancy is an advocate for the importance of spending quality time with our children. Not because of any consequences. Of all Nancy's accomplishments, she considers her daughter, now in her mid-twenties, her greatest blessing. In fact, Nancy considers having her daughter the best decision she's ever made. Yet older and wiser, Nancy realizes the effect our attention—given or neglected—can have on our children.

"It has really registered for me that every time we're looking at that screen or our children pick up on that flicker of distraction, they feel rejected. It hurts their self-esteem, and there are studies to prove it."

Yet giving our full attention to our children when we're also juggling a long to-do list is not easy. Part of that is a sense that we need to do it all, and we need to do it all at the same time. The end result? We're simply not present during our home time. This is something we inherently know yet don't consciously address.

"Not that long ago, I was at a baby shower, and we went around the room, sharing a lesson with the new mom. I went full-on lecture mode," Nancy recalls. "I'm sure it was the highlight of everyone's day," she says, laughing at herself. "But I really wanted to stress the point that *quality* time is so much more important than *quantity* time."

Having said that, if you think that you have to give up something to be the best parent you possibly can, that's simply not true. Nancy is living proof of this. From her position at Ogilvy and Mather, Nancy and her co-chief creative officer, Janet Kestin, cofounded Swim (swimprogram.ca), a leadership consultancy firm where they design programs that give ambitious individuals the tools they need to make their mark in the world. The duo has also cowritten two books, *Pick Me* and *Darling, You Can't Do Both (and Other Noise to Ignore on Your Way Up)*.

The point? You really can have it all: a career *and* a happy and healthy home life. You just need to remember that working hours belong in a different compartment in your brain from quality time with your children.

"One of the great things about being older," Nancy admits, "is that you get to say *learn from my mistakes*."

While today Nancy admits that even after their divorce, she and her former husband always put their daughter first, she also knows that she could have managed her attention better. This is something we're all guilty of and definitely something worth being aware of. It's important for our children as we help them build a healthy self-esteem. It's also important to do for ourselves, because while being a parent is a great responsibility, we also have a responsibility to our own dreams, aspirations, and purpose in life. The trick is in remembering that even our focus has a time and place—an inspiring lesson from one of our own, another superwoman who continues to live, learn, and share.

FOUR

IF YOU DON'T PAY ATTENTION, YOU PAY THE PIPER

IN THE BEGINNING . . . GOD was bored.

A wanderer, a drifter, an endless sigh, God spent most of Her time floating through Her solitary and hollow existence without a goal, without a purpose, without a real sense of awareness. With nothing to look forward to and nothing to look back upon, God seemed oblivious of Her own reason for being. She had no idea that a difference could be made; that the slightest change in her perspective could create an entire world. This was God's reality from the armpits of eternity.

Then it happened. God was hovering about, consumed by Her usual sense of disinterest, when suddenly, She was struck with an inkling of a vision and overtaken by inspiration. God immediately went to work. With an ambitious gathering of all Her breath and might, She began by transforming Her attitude of indifference into one of enthusiasm and anticipation. And She did this by inhaling the very moment in which She seemed to be stuck.

All at once, everything mattered to God, and with this new sense of caring came substance and density and a sense of now. God was overcome with a feeling to which She had never before paid attention. It was a feeling of being grounded. And so, She let Her essence surrender as She cascaded downward until Her being found mass. God named this new formation "the ground." Now directed with a sense of purpose, it was from this state of standing on a solid foundation that She continued to create Her entire world and purpose behind Her very existence.

Overwhelmed with all the feeling and a sudden sense of self-awareness and caring, God was soon overtaken by emotions She had never experienced before. This caused clarity to pour out of Her. And when this surge of emotional clarity came to an end, Her lips were transformed into a smile. No longer a linear sigh, this new burst of feeling and curve in her mouth inspired an idea. One of Her best ideas yet, She thought. Stirred by this clarity, She cast an intention, and suddenly bodies of water were filling the crevices of Her newly created ground. She called these oceans and lakes, ponds and streams. She made these bodies of water still and soaring and sometimes falling. With a smile on Her pleasant face, Her delight moved Her into a somersault. And at the moment that She reached upside down, Her smiling, inverted mouth became contagious, re-creating itself into a school of colorful arcs. Pinks and turquoise. Greens and yellows. She named these "rainbows" and, with a breath of intention, pursed her lips and blew until they scattered randomly about. Just then, the words "sky" and "wind" gently tumbled out of Her mouth, creating a textured and endless vastness.

There was no stopping God now. She went on to manifest mountains and minerals, vegetation and insects, animals and humans. She gave Her creatures instincts for survival and intelligence for progress. God even developed universal forces: some She named, like *Gravity* and *Cravings for Chocolate*; others She appointed as principles and kept secret. For the ones that She kept unnamed, She left clues for Her creatures to discover them. God's creative spree lasted an undetermined amount of time, until finally, She cut into the darkness, which then gave birth to light. Naming the separations "day" and "night," She entrusted to them the task of silent momentum, and together, day and night conceived differences in time that God called "what was," "what is," and "what shall be."

It was at this point that God wanted to take a moment to observe everything She had created. She decided to take a break and reflect. Her world had gone from hollow and void to brimming and abundant. Surrounded by colors and sounds, heartbeats and breaths, God allowed Herself a pause of nothing so that she could appreciate her labor. She called this moment "gratitude," folded it within the plush petals of a yellow rose, and gently placed it into a corner of her mind to be retrieved whenever She needed it. Gratitude, she realized, was a powerful force in itself.

Then God went to one of Her brand-new sandy beaches and, with a dirty martini in Her hand, walked on the edge of the water where salty waves changed the color of the sand, creating a fringed effect. Watching the lacey detail where wet and dry sand met, God was inspired by another idea. But just as She was about to create clothing for her human creatures, she was halted by a thought. Giving this thought words that included *creativity, independence,* and *manifestation,* She bestowed these onto her creatures as a gift. Clothing, She decided at that moment, would be up to Her human creatures to discover and design.

It was on this day, while God was lounging on one of Her beaches and blissfully sipping her martini, that Her world turned into mayhem. I'm not saying She let things get out of control. I'm just saying that a lot of shit went down that day.

Mayhem, you ask?

Yes. Mayhem. We've all had days like this.

Clashing storms appeared, bringing uncontrollable winds and rods of flashing light. Checking in on all of Her creations, from the smallest of insects to trees, animals, and humans, She observed their varying reactions with interest. As some scrambled for shelter with wide eyes and beating hearts, others expressed joy by dancing with the winds and swaying their leafy green happiness.

And then there was the hunger. Designed as a way to keep balance and order among Her darlings, God noticed that while some of Her creatures devoured their food with a great sense of pleasure, this caused other creatures to exist in a state of fear. In particular, Her humans seemed haunted by the tortured demise of their species as powerful, four-legged beasts preyed upon them.

But while the creatures in God's world reacted to the apparent chaos and eruptions, God wasn't completely worried, because just like all single mothers, God thinks of *everything*. She is always one thought ahead. You see, while God was creating the world, She knew that there would be life-threatening elements. Things like hindering weather conditions, hostile circumstances, and uncomfortable situations. And so, to equip Her darlings, God gave Her humans special abilities, including a strong sense of survival and an internal detector for sensing what she termed "red flags."

And to her sister single mothers, God gave an incredible source of strength. Sisters, you ask? Yes, of course, sisters. Because God, as the sole Creator of all things Earth and Life, feels a special connection to single mothers most of all. God, as the sole Creator of all, understands the challenges single mothers face. While single mothers have continuous mountains of laundry to tackle, God has mounds of ecosystems to maintain. Where single mothers are often the sole caretakers of their own creations, God has a deep sense of knowingness with no one to share or discuss it with.

You see, God, too, is alone in Her endeavors, and through Her own evolution from disinterest and a hollow existence, She's discovered that fear and the overwhelming can only be combated with courage, strength, and a sense of purpose. By developing a keen appreciation of awareness, She's learned that the only time She isn't filled with fear or dread is when

She is being true to Herself—perhaps the true definition of courage and strength.

And so, by infusing single mothers with especially sharp resources that include courage, outbursts of quasi-insanity, and quirks, along with a willingness to be the leaders of their own freak parades, single mothers most of all are bestowed with a superpower: the power of awareness. Watching out for signs defines not only our paths but our happiness and peace of mind. This is because Life is smarter than we are. Sometimes Life is busy cheering us on when we feel like no one else cares. Other times Life does her best to steer us away from danger. And when we're not paying attention, Life likes to mock us. Like all good friends do.

Questions of whether we're good enough will always haunt us. Issues will rise from the seeming quiet corners of our lives, and we'll wonder if we're doing the right thing. We'll get stuck in our heads and focus on matters that appear bigger than we are. But just as God did on that day when She was struck with an inkling of a vision and overtaken by inspiration, we have the power to turn our attention and change our perspectives. By paying attention to our own intuition and internal red flag detectors, we can veer from problems before they happen and create the most important thing of all: inner peace and contentment. Although not often recognized, this alone is a superpower.

This is important for ourselves first. The bonus is that it will naturally trickle into our children and throughout all aspects of the bubble that is our world—both inner and outer. All questions are answered by paying attention to the way we feel. The proof point for this is in our past. Think of a time when you ignored the red flag—that little voice that spoke to you—and the consequences that you endured because you didn't pay attention. You paid for that dearly, didn't you?

FIVE

HAVE YOU EVER BEEN BITTEN IN THE ASS BY YOUR OWN DECISIONS?

Did I put the clothes in the dryer?

Are the doors locked?

Crap! I forgot to get milk on my way home from work.

Why is it that we can lie awake at night listening to the incessant ramblings of the hamster, yet we don't listen to our own *feelings* (those damn red flags we choose to ignore, even when they're waving in our faces)? Decisions and choices always come with consequences—some good, others bad. We know this. Most of the time, we can actually feel when we're making a wrong decision. But do we listen to our feelings? Nope. We settle. We compromise. We ignore our own intuition. We make the stupid decision, even though that voice inside is yelling, "Don't do it! *Stop*! *Nooooooooooooo.*"

We do this so often that eventually that voice quietly gives up and morphs into a simple gesture: eye-rolling. At one point in my life, my voice got so good at eye-rolling that it remained in a permanent position of staring at my own spine. I could feel it, and it was uncomfortable. And yet I *chose* to ignore this too. The hard lesson here is that all of our decisions and choices really do have consequences. Yet it took me forever to grasp this. In hindsight, I became a single mom because I ignored the voice. All the red flags were there, and yet I chose to ignore them. This is that story.

When I was a kid, and before I even knew how procreation worked, I wasn't even going to have babies. Nope. I was going to have puppies. That being said, I've had both. I've had babies—four, to be precise—and I've had puppies. Lots and lots of puppies.

Both the babies and the puppies were decisions that I made. I'd wake up one morning and think, "I want a puppy," and by the end of that day, I was wiping up puddles of pee from the floor. (And swearing in regret.) More often than not, these decisions were not well thought out. In the case of puppies, sometimes it just wasn't a good time in my life. Unlike shaving your legs, puppies need daily attention, and sometimes this just isn't conducive to whatever else you have going on, like a job and long hours away from home and evenings where folding laundry, making supper, and helping kids with homework are the priorities. All of these take energy and time, and so does wiping up puppy pee from the floor.

In the case of babies, well, they *are* your life, so that's a different story. And while I have never had any regrets about having my babies, I didn't always make the right decision in terms of who I was going to have them with. Apparently, asking someone that you're hanging out with if they'd like to "go halfers on a baby" when you're nineteen years old is not what they mean by family planning. Don't judge me.

Looking back, the red flags were all there. All of them, lined up along the highway and screaming, "Not him! *Do not choose him*!" Well, instead of not choosing him (him being the father of my two eldest daughters), I chose to ignore the red flags. So how did this come about? Why did I decide to have children with a man who, thinking back, I knew wasn't the right choice? I'm not going to get psychoanalytical here (perhaps we'll save that for another chapter), but I will say this: I was young. I was naive. I was *stuuuuupid*. Here's how it all went down.

My first ventures into adulting took place over the span of living in a couple of apartments. The first was a one-bedroom in Lasalle, a suburb of Montreal, on the third floor of an apartment building right across the street from a McDonald's. I remember this well because McDonald's was a staple for me back then. How easy is it to walk across the street for a hamburger? Plus, back then, McDonald's was supercheap. I'm dating myself by remembering this, but the ads were about paying for your food and actually getting change back. (If you, too, remember those ads, we should probably hang out sometime.) When I wasn't eating a McDonald's quarter pounder with cheese, I was eating the same thing all week, because my idea of cooking back then was "if I'm taking the time to do this now, why not just make enough for the week?" I applied this rule of thumb to whatever I was cooking, whether it was macaroni casserole or pancake batter.

After losing that apartment for the sake of following a failed relationship across the country to Alberta, I moved back home to Lasalle, into the bachelor apartment of my mother's duplex. That kind of worked out, because while I was living "on my own," I could go upstairs and raid my mother's fridge whenever I got hungry.

It was during this time that I met a young adulting boy—the one who would become the person I went halfers on babies with. Notice I'm not calling him the father of my children. There's a reason for that, which I'm about to share with you. Going forward, we will refer to this person as Mr. What-Was-I-Thinking. At the time, I was nineteen years old, and he was twenty-two. He was still living at home and didn't have a job. *(Red flag number 1. Ignored.)*

To clarify, "home" meant his parents' house. Now I'm not saying that there's anything wrong with a twenty-two-year-old living with his parents. In fact, if I could go back in time, I would have lived at home until I completely and confidently felt ready to live on my own. Which, if I'm to be perfectly honest, would be sometime today, preferably after I've had lunch.

I had been seeing Mr. What-Was-I-Thinking for several weeks when he went into the hospital to have a knee operation. Nothing serious that I can remember, and I know this because the last I heard, he was still walking by using said knee. It was during this time that I had one of my great ideas. And by great, I mean stupid. To give you context, his bedroom at his parents' house was in the basement. I, being the I-can-save-the-world type of person back then (insert eye-rolling), said to him, "Hey, why don't you stay with me in my one-room bachelor apartment until your knee gets better?"

And that was the beginning of him never leaving.

This is in no way a male-bashing session, but I will say this: it was during our five years together that I was introduced, by my mother, to the word *opportunist,* which is the word she used when referring to Mr. What-Was-I-Thinking. If I was naive to a fault, he was sinfully irresponsible. Admittedly, I was irresponsible as well. I not only chose to have babies with this unlikely candidate. I also chose to have babies when I should have been focusing on my future, specifically, my career. At the time, having babies should have been the last thing on my mind—even more last than having puppies. At the time, I was working as a customer service representative for a magazine company. My job was to handle subscription issues. Soon, I was promoted to customer service manager, which, looking back, tells me that I had potential—even as far back as then—potential that I wish I would have recognized. But instead, I decided—I *chose*—to have babies with a man who would turn out to be about as good at fathering as some people are at running countries. (Oops. Did I say that out loud?)

Up until having babies, I would have described our relationship as quasi-brand-new with no hope for a future. Everything changed when we had babies, in that Mr. What-Was-I-Thinking stayed the same (unemployed), whereas I began to realize that stuff needed to get done. Stuff like saving money to maybe one day buy a house. Or to buy diapers. The fighting also changed. Instead of fighting with Mr. What-Was-I-Thinking, I now fought with myself. The arguments went something like this:

ME: I don't love him.
ALSO ME: But I *have* to love him.
ME: Why do I have to love him?
MY RESPONSE TO ME: Because you have babies with him.

This argument was a losing battle, because either way, I lost: either I stayed with a man whom I did not love and lived in an unhappy family environment, or I left said man and became a single mother. I chose the latter.

Now, about those decisions and the consequences of those decisions. I knew Mr. What-Was-I-Thinking wasn't the "one." And yet I *chose* to have babies with him. As I write about this and remember those days, I'm imagining that you know what I'm going to say next: life was not easy. In fact, it was downright hard. I was young. So damn young. I still didn't have it all figured out. And after we broke up, I had no support from Mr. What-Was-I-Thinking (hence the reason why *father* and *daddy* don't play a big role in his description).

The upside to all this is that I got to raise two wonderful little girls in the deal. And in raising them, I, too, grew up. Our time together? I wouldn't change a single thing. Yes, I struggled to put food on the table, and most days felt like Life was trying to bite my ass, but looking back now, I wish I could get some of those days back. Times were tough, but those years also held a lot of magic. Looking back, I realize now that many of my problems stemmed from defining myself by my status of "single mother." This was a big mistake, and one that I encourage you to avoid. You see, I wasn't just a single mother. I was a young adult with a lot of potential.

But focusing on my status ate away at some of my best years. Bad decisions do not define us. They make great stories. What's done is done, and the only thing we can do is learn and move on. Let me repeat that: learn and move on. Which is the complete opposite of dwell and stay stuck.

The biggest takeaway here is that our decisions really do come with a price tag. And yet we make decisions every single day of our lives. We will make bad decisions (learning experiences), and we'll make great decisions. The important thing is to *listen* to how you feel as you're making those decisions.

Make sense?

SIX

FROM WHERE YOU ARE TO WHERE YOU WANT TO BE WITH THE THREE CS

WHEN A MOTHER LEAVES THE hospital with her new baby, she's given a "mommy starter kit." This care package comes complete with formula coupons, a few diaper samples from the big brands, forms to fill out so that the differing departments of the government are aware of its new citizen, and brochures on topics like car seats and breastfeeding. Did I say this package comes *complete*? Let me rephrase that, because information on one topic is never given to a mother, regardless of whether she's a first-time or seasoned mom—instructions on how to nurture *herself,* her potential, her dreams, and her aspirations. As mothers, we become givers, champions of all the trials and tribulations of parenting—one trial and tribulation at a time. It's a learning curve. One that lasts the rest of our lives.

While being a mom is perhaps the most important role you will ever play in another human being's life, you'll do a much better job at it if you put yourself first and foremost and take care that *your* needs are met—from how you feel about the way you look to the things that make your heart sing. This includes hobbies (reading?), passions (making jewelry?), plans for a bright future (owning a home one day?), and a good haircut.

I'm saying this here because, again, I wish someone had told me this when I was a young single mother.

Looking back at younger me, twenty-four years old was really the verge of adulthood. That's how old I was when I decided that I'd had enough. It was a tremulant time. I was dissatisfied with my life. Unhappy. Neither the present nor the future had meaning. At the time, I was living with Mr. What-Was-I-Thinking, the father of my two daughters. Why do I call him that? While I was working my ass off to pay the bills and put food on "our" table, he was living the good life. In this context, the good life is about not worrying about anything. Like when you're twelve years old and life is simple and carefree. Mr. What-Was-I-Thinking didn't take work or earning a living seriously. Everything fell on me. Holy realization, Batman! *I was living with a freaking twelve-year-old!*

But wait! Before I get too hard on myself, let's remember that I, too, was young.

Mr. What-Was-I-Thinking had a pattern. He would work for a few months at a job he enjoyed complaining about, then get fired or quit and maybe go on unemployment insurance if he had stuck it out long enough to qualify. I have a very vivid memory of him sitting in the baby pool in our backyard, hippy bandana wrapped around his head, beer in his hand, and that's how he spent his summers while I went to work every day. At the time, I was young, naive, and, quite frankly, too busy and exhausted to notice how ridiculous it all was.

The final straw came one evening after I'd just tucked in our two young daughters for the night. They were three years and six months old at the time. I was sitting in a chair, reading, and I could hear him, Mr. What-Was-I-Thinking, walking around the house snapping his fingers. He hadn't told me yet, but he was getting ready to go out. It was his finger-snapping that told me. You see, he had this thing, this damn unconscious pattern. Whenever he was excited about some big plans to "go out with the boys," he would walk around the house, snapping his fingers. *Snap, snap.* (I fucking hated that sound, and still do, as I listen to the echo in my brain as I write this.)

Then he snapped his way over to where I was sitting in the living room and asked if I had twenty dollars. According to his "big plans for the evening," twenty dollars was precisely the amount of money he needed to have a much-needed night out. Even though he'd had much-needed nights out every single week.

"It's my last twenty dollars, and I have to buy formula for the baby tomorrow," I said. Thinking back, I didn't just "say" those words; I pleaded them. Like pleading a case. Like begging.

"But I need it to get into the bar tonight. I'll borrow it off someone and give it back to you tomorrow," he promised. *Pfft.* Reluctantly, I went into my wallet, pulled out the last twenty I had to my name until my next paycheck, and gave it to him. I didn't feel good about doing this and consoled myself by returning my attention to the book I was reading.

Soon after, I heard the water running. He was taking a shower, getting ready for his "big night out." (Yes, I just rolled my eyes at the memory.) That night had just cost me. Not only was I out my last twenty dollars, but now I needed to worry about how I was going to afford to buy baby formula. Then the phone rang. It was his friend, Glenn, the one he was going out with, and a little voice in my head told me that this would be a good time to chat him up. It was perhaps the best advice that little voice had ever given me.

"So," I said as I lay my book on my lap and dug my shoulders further into the back of the faux leather chair. Thinking back, I think that in my heart of hearts, I knew the truth and positioned my body to hear it. "I heard it costs twenty dollars to get in tonight." It sounded like a statement, but really it was a question. Glenn's response?

"Oh, not for us. It's my father's event, so there's no charge."

I kept my cool, but really, I was seething under the chitchat. All my brain could compute was that, one, Mr. What-Was-I-Thinking had just lied to me; two, I told him that it was my last twenty dollars and that the baby needed formula; and three, fuck. *Fuck. Fuck. Fuck.* I felt the sting from the truth as though someone had slapped me across the face. Mr. What-Was-I-Thinking was a liar. A damn liar. Of course, it wasn't the first time. I knew it. I ignored it. I tried to create a better truth. But even that was a lie. Looking back, I remember myself as a slow learner. Or possibly just hopeful that Mr. What-Was-I-Thinking would one day grow up and be the family man I needed him to be. This was the night the truth broke free, and I had no choice but to face it.

After Mr. What-Was-I-Thinking left that night, I stayed seated on that chair for the longest time and thought about our situation. The longer I thought, the more I realized that it wasn't "our" situation; it was *my* situation. And I needed to make some changes in the way of wanting more for myself and my little girls. Instead of feeling sorry for myself or wishing he had stayed home with me, I allowed myself to get angry. The kind of angry that bends you out of shape and triggers the kind of vengeance that comes from the Satan part of your core. Confession: I went a little crazy that night.

Going through the house, I gathered every single one of his belongings and threw them out on the front lawn. His clothes? *Out.* His records? *Out.* His toothbrush and razor? *Out.* The big chest filled with all his crap in our bedroom? *All out.*

Meanwhile, a question was spinning in my brain: *How the hell did I get here?* Sometimes the emphasis was on the word *I.* (How could this happen to *me?*) Sometimes the emphasis was on the word *here.* (Time had stopped, and I was on the edge of a cliff, as though my life were over.)

Regardless, it was always the same question, and eventually I came to the realization that I needed to fix this. I needed a plan. The first thing on my agenda was to make it official by getting Mr. What-Was-I-Thinking's name off the lease of the house we were renting. This was not his home anymore. He was not going to sponge off me or deprive our—*my*—kids ever again.

The next morning, I called the landlord and made an appointment to see him. I was on a mission. There was no turning back now. I would not let myself. I *could not* let myself. Not for the sake of my sanity and not for the sake of my future. I was leaving him for *me,* and if there's one thing I've learned about human nature, it's that once you realize that *you* are more important than the crappy situation you're in, there really is no turning back. That realization was the stepping-stone I needed to make the change I was too afraid to face.

I would never have admitted this back then, but I'll tell you now: I was determined, but I was also filled with fear. If life was hell living as a couple—as a so-called family—what was it going to be like as a single mother? How many doors was I closing for myself? As you can imagine, ending up as a single mother was not what I had planned for myself. I felt like the odds were against me. I felt like Life Herself was against me.

Even before that night—that important milestone of a night—and before the decision to take back control of my life, I felt overwhelmed *all the time.* Getting my girls ready in the morning. Taking them to the day care. Hopping back on a bus to get to my job, praying all the while that I would arrive on time. Rushing back to the day care to pick up my girls. Getting home and making supper. My life was an endless swirl of to-dos and responsibilities. I remember waking up in the middle of the night, feeling like my heart was going to explode. I was consumed with anxiety. Even *with* Mr. What-Was-I-Thinking, I felt alone. And now, I didn't even have the pretense of my "family," regardless of how fake and crappy it actually was.

On the morning of my appointment with the landlord, I woke up feeling both scared and determined. Our meeting was at his office, and while I was sitting in the waiting room, all I could think was, what if he won't accept the lease change? What if he instead cancels the lease and makes me move? I didn't have money to pay movers. All these thoughts were rolling in my head until finally the landlord came out of his office to greet me. As I watched him walk down the hall toward me, every ounce of my being was focused on remaining calm. Poker face. No expression. Determined to "win."

I'll never forget what I was wearing that day: a pair of lilac slacks, a white blouse, and black high-heeled shoes. I was dressed like another day at the office, but I felt like a ninja, and I wasn't going to take shit from anyone. My mood was fierce. I was not leaving that office without a new lease in my name. Then, just as he reached a few feet in front of me, his hand beginning to extend into a handshake, I took a deep breath and stood up slowly. I knew that with those heels, I'd be taller than him, and I wanted to make sure to intimidate him in some small way. I towered over him. Our eyes met, and he smiled nervously. The moment didn't last long—just long enough for me to know that I had had an effect on him. Precisely what I had intended.

Something changed in me that day. It was the day I realized that for everything I wanted in life, only one person could get it, and that person was me. I also realized that for everything I wanted in life, only one person could get in my way: also me. I was scared; I needed *courage*. I was doubtful; I needed *confidence*. I was dissatisfied; I needed to make a *commitment* to my decision to want more from life.

That very day, I realized that these three things—courage, confidence, and commitment—were all things that I had control over. Hell, after what I had just gone through with

Mr. What-Was-I-Thinking—the loss of control, the whirl-wind of always living in lack and deprivation—leaving him took courage. It took confidence. And it took a commitment to myself for a better life. This was a good lesson in taking back control, and I knew I was on the right path and that I would be okay. My tools—my power—was in these three Cs: Courage. Confidence. Commitment.

I learned quite a few things from that experience. I learned that there's a difference between being alone and being lonely. I was terribly lonely in my relationship with Mr. What-Was-I-Thinking. By myself? I was in control. I was alone, but I also learned that I could be happy. I observed that the world only treats you as well as you treat yourself. If you treat yourself with respect, others will as well. If you feel you deserve success, whatever that means to you, you will achieve it. This is because Life gives you what you believe you deserve. Please read that last sentence again. There's truth there, and once you understand it, doors will open for you.

Homework: Get up, right now, and go look at yourself in the mirror. Look into your own eyes and say the words: *Life gives you what you believe you deserve. And I deserve to be happy, damn it!*

Do it. Feel it. Know it. Believe it. Now grow from it.

MARGERY BAGLEY WELCH

*Thoughts on grace as a superpower
in dealing with obstacles*

MARGERY WAS THIRTY-NINE YEARS OLD when she first became a single mother. Her daughter and son, six and seven years old at the time, still belonged to an age of naïveté and trust. Especially trust of adults. And while Margery spent much of her time maneuvering through her many tasks and responsibilities, as most single mothers do, she had a few extra challenges to deal with, the first occurring about three years after the end of her marriage, when her daughter was diagnosed with a genetic disorder, causing her to be legally blind.

"When my daughter was first diagnosed, I was scared. Up until that point, I had had two healthy children, and all of a sudden one of them had a visual impairment that was going to affect her for the rest of her life. I needed to help her, and I had no idea how I was going to do that. I felt helpless," Margery says, thinking back.

At the time, her former husband was going through

something that looked a lot like a midlife crisis, leaving Margery to deal with this abrupt change on her own. She spent many hours reading up on the disorder, as well as researching federal government agencies that could assist with equipment requirements and training.

"I was also worried about her college education and didn't know if I could get her into a school that would give her access to everything she needed. I even looked into programs for visually impaired students. Things I would have usually taken for granted, such as the school environment and how she would be set up. These had become very real concerns."

To Margery's disappointment, she was left to deal with these issues on her own. And nothing knows the heavy lonesomeness of facing life challenges like the shoulders of a single mother.

The second obstacle to be put on Margery's path was her former husband's new girlfriend. As mothers, putting our children first is priority number one. We guard their health and safety like lionesses; sometimes raw with emotion, other times baring our teeth in anger to anyone who poses an unkind threat—big or small. This is both part of our job as parents and natural in the way that we've been designed to co-create. We're humans. We're animals. We know our place and will do anything to protect our loved ones. Yet there's a fine line between our humanity and our instincts. Often, taming our own nature is the best way to handle a situation. Margery's story demonstrates this well.

There's an expression: you never get a second chance at making a first impression. And when Margery met her former husband's girlfriend for the first time, the impression was a good one, although deceiving. The new girlfriend was polite and even took an interest in the well-being of their children. As single mothers, we know how important this is. While we can't be with our children 24/7, there's comfort in knowing that when we can't be there, the people whom they're with are taking our children's care to heart.

Slowly at first, the truth began to seep out. It started when the kids were visiting their father. The schedule, set prior to him meeting his new girlfriend, was that the parental visits with their father occurred every second weekend and one evening every week. Suddenly there was a new rule: the children were not permitted to contact their mother while visiting with their father; they were not even allowed to respond to Margery's texts. And as Margery would find out later, when her kids were at their father's, the girlfriend would make snide comments to them about their mother.

Concerning Margery's daughter and her health issues, the girlfriend would interject and openly express what she felt Margery was doing wrong or neglecting to do. The girlfriend even insisted on being included in meetings with specialists for her daughter's needs, including with doctors and school authorities.

"There was one incident during the winter months when I took the kids in for their annual physicals and when the results came back from their routine blood tests, the doctor found that their vitamin D was lower than she would have liked," recalls Margery. "It wasn't an issue. The doctor said that it was normal for that time of year since most people spend more time indoors than during the summer months, and she recommended that I give the kids vitamin D chocolate chews, one in the morning and one at night. After purchasing the chocolate chews, I arrived home to find my ex-husband at my home to pick up the kids. I shared the doctor's recommendation with him, and he took the supplements so that he could give them to the kids while they were with him.

"I received a call from him later that evening, telling me that his girlfriend didn't feel the kids needed to take the supplements. I remember at the time starting to feel that she was trying to discredit everything I did or said concerning the kids."

As you can imagine, Margery was in a difficult situation.

She wanted to uphold her role as mother and primary care-giver to her children while maintaining a good relationship with her former husband. This is when Margery started to realize what was going on: her former husband had gotten involved with a controlling woman, and even he wasn't able to stand up to her. This problem lasted for about seven years, until the couple eventually broke up. Seven years is a long time when you're constantly trying to calm a frustrating situation while maintaining your ground.

"Luckily, I didn't have to see her that often," admits Margery. "She never spoke to me directly. When she had a message for me, she would tell my ex-husband. And if I disagreed with it, which I often did, I would just tell him, 'No. This is how it's going to be.' And I would then proceed with whatever plan my ex-husband and I had agreed upon in terms of dealing with the situations concerning our children."

Margery was relentless in her capacity to stay true to herself and to her children. Yet the situation persisted.

"I realized just how bad it was one day when my son came home from school and I could tell that something was very wrong. It took some time for me to get the story out of him, but when I did, that's when I realized that not only was this woman controlling but she was not particularly nice to my kids.

"It was one morning just before school, and because of her bad knees, she had asked my son to go upstairs where the cat's litter box was to clean it out. Just as my son was finishing up with the litter box, she climbed the stairs to check on what kind of job he had done, and the words from her mouth cut into him: 'You didn't do it right! What are you, some kind of an asshole?'"

Margery, a woman dealing with the demands of single motherhood, topped with a child facing debilitating health issues and her ex-husband's controlling and even venomous live-in girlfriend, managed to stand her ground. With grace.

With compassion. And with a strength that even she didn't know she possessed when her journey as a sole parent began.

As superwomen, we're often presented with trying times. And as Margery learned, patience and an ability to maintain composure are often the best tools in our arsenal of weapons.

With so much to deal with in terms of frustration, it would have been easy to get more involved in the antics of a controlling woman. Confrontation can be a form of stress relief yet would only have added to the negative circumstances and impact on her kids.

Kudos to you, Margery.

SEVEN

ABOUT TENNIS SOCKS, AND WHY YOU SHOULD NEVER, EVER STUFF THEM IN YOUR BRA

IT'S PRETTY SAFE TO SAY that at some point, we've all done something stupid. Something that at the time seemed like a great idea. These *great ideas* usually strike us in such a way that they temporarily knock common sense right out of us the same way that a punch in the stomach leaves us breathless. Right now, I'm imagining that you're thinking about some of the dumb things you've done and nodding your head in agreement.

As I write this, I can't help but think about my friend Patricia, who woke up one morning and decided that she needed to drive to her boyfriend's house to throw eggs at his car. I don't remember the reason—something to do with stalking him on Facebook during a middle-of-the-night insomnia fest and noticing that he liked just about everything his ex-wife had posted. After she told me the story, we both agreed that while throwing eggs at his car made her feel better, it really was a stupid thing to do. Especially since her boyfriend was a cop.

I tell you this not because it's part of my plan for this chapter but to feel better about myself, because the story I'm about to share with you deems me the queen of doing stupid things. As you may have guessed from the title of this chapter, I put tennis socks in my bra. Once. In my defense, young girls across the globe have been stuffing their bras since the bra's invention. Although I was in my late thirties at the time. Don't judge me.

But I learned something from said stupid thing. For example, I learned that I needed to do something about my self-confidence. I also learned how I felt about my relationship with the rest of the world, and by the rest of the world, I mean the two men sitting at the next table.

To put this time of my life into context, I had just turned thirty-seven years old and was living in a house full of people. Almost like a cult, except that I was related to these people, and none of us ever drank Kool-Aid. The cult members comprised my at-the-time partner in crime, our two toddlers, my two daughters from a previous relationship, and his daughter from a previous relationship. Mine and his equaled ours, and we were a household of seven humans and various other creatures: four dogs, two goats, a cat, three birds, and, quite frequently, my mother when she came to visit. (Just to clarify, I am in no way referring to my mom as a creature.)

At the time of this particular memory, it was wintertime, and my ex—we'll call him Peter—had suddenly become enamored by the cold weather we Canadians refer to as hell. I knew this from his sudden interest in snowmobiling. Just kidding. No one really appreciates the cold weather and all the shivering and swearing that go along with it. Riding around on a snowmobile (which is basically a motorcycle with skis) is just a way for some of us to *pretend* that we enjoy the crappy, frigid weather that belongs to the longest season of the northern hemisphere.

In those days, Peter liked to take off on long rides on Saturday afternoons, only to return at the end of the day with rosy cheeks and a happy face. One evening, during dinner, he spoke about the snowmobile "clubhouse" that he had discovered deep in the woods, and he told me about all the new friends he had made. I'm not sure why I started thinking about this, but suddenly I had visions of him hanging out at this "clubhouse" with gorgeous waitresses. (Except in my mind, they looked like voluptuous go-go girls in high boots and miniskirts. It seemed my imagination had been hijacked by the 1960s.)

Although I had no interest in the fine sport of freezing my ass off, I suddenly became driven by curiosity and decided that I needed to check out this new interest for myself.

"Hey! How about taking me out for lunch?" I said to him one Saturday morning (after checking the weather to make sure I wouldn't die from frostbite).

"Sure," he said. "Where would you like to go?"

My response? "The clubhouse."

At this point, I had no idea that I was about to cross a line and go from the type of woman who teaches her children about self-acceptance and a positive body image to voracious bra stuffer. The idea to stuff tennis socks into my bra came to me at exactly 11:15 that morning. I remember this because I was folding laundry on the kitchen table (and yes, matching tennis socks was a big part of this task) when Peter walked in to ask if I'd be ready to leave at noon. My eyes darted from the clock on the stove down to the sweatpants that I was wearing when I realized *I need to change!*

"Where are you going?" he asked.

"To get ready!" I yelled back as I took the stairs two at a time toward our bedroom.

Tearing through our closet, I just couldn't seem to find the right outfit. I wanted to look casual yet stunning. My red Marilyn Monroe dress . . . simple, black cocktail dress . . . nothing—*nothing*—was appropriate for a stupid ride on a snowmobile! Shuffling hangers like a madwoman on thirteen cups of coffee, it wasn't until I finally reached the sweater section of my closet that I realized I still had a tennis sock in my hand. Hmm . . . coincidence? I thought not. I flew down the stairs to get the matching sock—or not, whatever, just another sock matching in size would do—and as I was heading back upstairs, Peter appeared with my snowsuit. *My hardly ever worn snowsuit.*

"Here," he said. "I dug this out for you. You'll need it. It's cold out there."

Semi-matching sock in hand, I took the suit and ran back upstairs.

"I'll be ready in twenty minutes," I yelled to the walls, counting on them to ricochet my voice without the panic. Back in our room, I put on my snuggest-fitting jeans, stuffed the socks into my bra, and squeezed myself into the tightest sweater I could find. In fact, I'm pretty sure it wasn't even my sweater but one that had made its way into my closet instead of that of its rightful owner—one of my teenage daughters.

Not wanting Peter or any of our kids to see my new double-D boobs, I put the snowsuit on and, feeling much like what I imagined an astronaut feels like walking on the moon—excited and both light and heavy at the same time—I ambled my way downstairs to announce that I was ready for our lunch at the clubhouse.

As I suspected, the snowmobile ride was cold and miserable. Also long. Very, very long. As I learned later, Peter misunderstood my sudden interest and motive for enthusiasm and decided to take the scenic route to the clubhouse. Oh joy, oh freaking bliss.

Have you ever ridden on a snowmobile? Let me tell you that feigning zeal through gritting, shivering teeth is less fun than it sounds. Also, there's a lot of jiggling and jaggling going on from parts of your body that you didn't even know could jiggle and jaggle. This, from the vibration of the snowmobile. Oh, and there's swearing. A lot of swearing. Especially when the ice-cold wind crashes into your face. One of the great mysteries of the world is how people enjoy the outdoors during winter months.

Finally, we arrived at the clubhouse. I wasn't sure what to expect, but I was ready. *Crunch, crunch, crunch,* Peter and I walked through the snow toward an old, log-house, chalet-type building, and as we walked in, I was accosted by the sound of men talking and laughing. Lots and lots of men. As we stood in the doorway and looked around for a table, I quickly noticed that one thing was missing from this environment: hot babes. To be more specific, *the* hot babes I had imagined. Deciding to let my boyfriend take the lead, I followed him to a table. Silently, I thanked a warmhearted god for the empty table close to the roaring fire.

We set our helmets down on the chairs around our table and started to undress. Gloves, hats, scarves, snowsuits unzipped and pulled down to our waists, we settled in for an intimate lunch date. Peering over the menu, I looked around once again to make sure I hadn't missed anything (I was still on hot babe alert and feeling very insecure), and lo and behold, I noticed that the men sitting a few tables away from us were staring at me. *Me!* More specifically, they were staring at my big, bosomy, tennis sock–infested chest.

"Peter!" I whispered in excitement. "Men are looking at my chest! No one *ever* looks at my chest."

"Um, yeah. What's going on with those, anyway?" Peter asked.

Looking down, I realized why my female figure of magnetism was attracting stares. It was not due to my voluptuous physique but rather to my lopsided chest. The damn snowmobile ride had misplaced my socks. Well, not both, but one. The sock in my left cup had escaped and had settled just above my solar plexus. And very noticeably, thanks to my skin-tight sweater. I looked like a boob job gone completely wrong. Hunchback of Notre Abdomen.

While part of me wanted to reach under my sweater to fetch the runaway sock and throw it at the men at the next table, another part of me realized that once again, I was ridiculous in my need for security and acceptance. I mean seriously, tennis socks in my bra? What was I thinking?

I never put tennis socks in my bra again. Although once in a while, I do think about the possibility of getting a boob job.

EIGHT

TODAY IS NOT A STEPPING-STONE TO TOMORROW—PLEASE DON'T TREAT IT AS ONE

WE'RE ALL GUILTY OF SOME variation of this:

I'll be happy with myself after I lose ten pounds.

I'll love my home when I get out of this apartment and move into a "real house."

I'd enjoy my job more if my boss weren't such an asshole.

For me, it was that life would be easier once my kids were older. In hindsight, this was one of the stupidest string of words ever to chase each other inside my brain. And the worst part is that I actually believed that once my kids got older, life would be easier. Looking back, I now realize that I was robbing myself—and my kids—of the here and now: the precious moments that become carved into our minds, giving us the history that creates the whole of our existence.

When my younger children, who are a year less thirteen days apart, were one and two years old, I couldn't wait for them to be two and three. Then, when we were celebrating their third and fourth birthdays, I fantasized about how great life was going to be when they turned four and five—old enough for day care. Then, when they were old enough for day care, I couldn't wait for them to be older so that they could make their own breakfast.

Looking back, this is one of my biggest fails as a parent: I didn't fully appreciate every age, stage, and coming of age. Of course, it wasn't all wishing the years away. There were times when I seized the moment and loved the hell out of the here and now. When I close my eyes and quiet the incessant voices in my head, I can still hear the way my son laughed when he was two and thought something was the funniest thing he'd ever seen (like me popping my head up from just below his vision while he sat in his highchair—"peekaboo!"). Or the look of pride on my youngest daughter's face as she deliberately yet cautiously took her first steps—even back then, I could see the wisdom emanating from her tiny, beaming countenance, well aware that she was doing something special. Or the feeling that all was right in the world as I listened to the rhythmic breathing of my sleeping babies when I checked in on them before retiring to my own bed at the end of a long day.

But for the most part, I wanted my kids to be older. More independent. Self-sufficient. When my kids were young and I was less mature, I thought life would get simpler as they got older, that I would be "happier" if I had less on my shoulders. Today I think back and yearn for the days when they were still mine. As I write this, my kids are thirty-two, twenty-nine, twenty, and nineteen years old, and I realize that even though life was harder when they were children, toddlers, and babies, there was a lot of perfection in those moments, regardless of the struggles.

My single mother days can be divided into two separate chunks of time. I fondly remember the first as the Trio Era. It began when I was twenty-four years old, and the trio consisted of my two eldest daughters and myself. This era ended when I was thirty-two; this was when I met Peter, the father of my two youngest children. So technically, I was on my own with my girls for eight years, and during most of those years, I didn't have a car, so the girls and I spent a lot of time on the city bus. The city bus was our ride to the grocery store, the day care, my job—everywhere. Living in NDG (a suburb of Montreal) for much of that time, the bus was our means of transportation.

At the time of this memory, the girls and I lived at the end of a dead-end street, next to a train track. Our two-bedroom apartment was on the third floor of a six-apartment building that had no elevator and two apartments on each floor. The building was small enough to be quaint, but since the street was lined with other similar apartment buildings, the neighborhood was also random enough to be filled with strangers. The buildings were detached, and so were their residents. The girls and I lived in that building for about two years, beginning when my daughters were three and six years old, and I spoke a lot to them about "strangers" and why one must never, ever speak to them.

We were walking down our street to the bus stop, and as we passed an older Italian woman who I assumed was a widow since she was dressed in black, I remember holding my girls' hands protectively, pulling them in closer to my sides. Then, on the bus on our way to their school and day care, someone would look down and smile at them, and I'd pull them in close to me and remind them again, "Don't talk to strangers." I was obsessed with keeping my kids safe, and at the time, it seemed that our every movement was imposed by the shadows of, you guessed it, strangers.

As I write this, I realize that part of my wishing for my kids to be older had nothing to do with wanting a simpler life and more to do with fear. Their safety was my sole responsibility, and I was terrified of something bad happening to them. I felt like a 24/7 guard dog in a junkyard. Not that my life or my kids were a junkyard but rather that there was just so much stuff to watch out for that it became hard to know where to put my focus. As a result, I just guarded it all, all the time, with bared teeth and watchful eyes. Look at my kids and yes, my glare will snap at you.

It wasn't until my eldest daughter was in her twenties that she confessed something to me about those days, something I had never considered before. We were having dinner together at a restaurant, just the two of us, when she said to me, "Do you remember how you used to tell us all the time 'don't talk to strangers'? Well, I didn't understand that. I didn't know what a stranger was."

That's when I realized that throughout all my paranoia and dark fantasies of my kids being kidnapped by a random serial killer, I had never taken the time to explain to them exactly what a stranger actually was . . . is. (Possibly a good thing, because statistics have since revealed that most "bad people"—the kind who do unthinkable things to children— are either our relations or our neighbors.)

And here's the thing: while I was so busy worrying about my children's safety, and wishing that they were older, fanta-sizing about the future and its promise of easier days, I shortchanged myself on two things. Let's start with the obvious: the moments of the here and now. Today I realize that life is not about the destination; it's about the journey. It's about the days and ages of your kids that you can never get back. It's about the laughter and the first steps and the joyful routine of nights that get safely tucked in at the end of a day, and the sense of safety that you hear from rhythmic breathing. The long days and never-ending to-do lists are where magic happens, no matter how tired or overwhelmed or defeated we feel at the time. Even this moment—that precise moment that just slipped by as you read the last word of this sentence—is a moment lost forever. It's like melted ice cream at the bottom of a bowl. You can see it was there, the evidence sits unassumingly, but the tasty goodness is gone. Gone forever. And unless you were focusing on the creamy coldness between the roof of your mouth and your tongue and the savory decadence of double chocolate chip, all you're left with is a bowl that needs to be washed and shelved.

The less obvious loss of not appreciating the moment in the moment is regret, but perhaps not for the reasons that you're thinking. The truth is that as our children get busy growing up into their own, they, too, become strangers as they slip into their place in the world. Their lives take on a meaning and purpose that has nothing to do with you anymore. And unless you're paying attention at the time and appreciating the little things, those moments get lost forever.

The tiny heartfelt voice that says "I yuv you, Mommy" eventually changes to a quip: "Love you, Ma."

The little feet with shoelaces that need tying grow into independent steps that spend more time walking away from you than toward you.

The evening ritual of bath, teeth brushing, and bedtime stories eventually dries up to nights spent looking up at the ceiling as you wait with bated breath for teenagers to walk through the front door, safe and unharmed.

I often speak about the importance of remembering who you are. A parent, yes. But regardless of labels and statuses, you are an individual with an inherent need for purpose and recognition. But not at the expense of wishing today away for a tomorrow that has no legs. Every experience, every version of your former self, every stage of life—they really are all important. It's especially important to maintain a friendly and open relationship with every single one of the "yous" of days and years past, but you can't do that if you're not paying attention. Have your dreams, look forward to your tomorrows, but remember that today is the true gift.

To remind myself, I have the words "Right here, right now" tattooed on my forearm. True story.

VIRGINIA SMITH

Thoughts on being a teenage mother

INNER STRENGTH CAN BE AS powerful as it is silent, and as tenacious as it is resilient. Often, we're not even aware of its existence or, especially, that we ourselves are in possession of the inner strength we admire in others. Hollywood likes to make movies about people who overcome extraordinary circumstances: people like Erin Brockovich, Chris Gardner, and Patch Adams. For some reason, it seems almost *human nature* to look at others and oooh and ahhhh over their achievements despite great obstacles that seem bigger than they are. What we see is the magnitude of their persistence, and their capacity to prevail against the odds that stand like a great wall, abrupt and unyielding, in their path.

And yet we—yes, you and I—often don't recognize this inner strength in ourselves. The truth about inner strength is that as determined as it is, it is subtle—a series of baby steps as we manage one challenge at a time while feeling as though we're being pulled underwater by unseen hands. In the midst of it all, we think we're drowning and feel like failures. And then we surprise ourselves.

Virginia was seventeen years old when she became a mother. Still in high school at the time, she felt that she needed to keep her "condition" a secret. She was in an accelerated program that was designed to prepare students for college, and since her education had always been her priority, Virginia was afraid of getting expelled from the program.

"You couldn't be pregnant in the program, so I had to hide it. I hid my pregnancy from the public and from myself," Virginia admits today. "I realize now that I was having trouble coming to terms with the fact that I was going to have a baby."

Anyone who has ever been seventeen years old will agree: no longer a child yet not quite equipped for the demands of adulting, the teenage years are a confusing time. A perspective that hasn't fully developed simply because of limited life experiences. An overload of hormonal changes. An unclear, and even baffling, sense of self-awareness. These are just some of the reasons why most of us would prefer not to step into the time machine that brings us back to when we were seventeen. Throw in the daunting realization that you're pregnant, and it may seem like your young life is on its way to falling off a cliff.

Although Virginia did graduate from high school, she didn't attain the special certificate for which she had worked so hard. Despite all her efforts to complete high school while striving to hide her pregnancy, she went into labor during the final days of her graduating year and missed an important exam. This was Virginia's first taste of the consequences of her circumstances. Although she was devastated, she still had all intentions to further her education.

"I ended up applying to the university in my hometown of Daytona Beach," Virginia recalls. "It's where I grew up, and everyone knew me, so I just called the school and I got into the chemistry program within two days."

Not being familiar with or aware of the different government programs designed to help single mothers attain their education, Virginia paid her own way through college with the help of some inheritance money that afforded her the day care services she needed, as well as through the help of a full scholarship that she had earned. To manage the other living expenses required for supporting herself and her daughter, Virginia worked at a local grocery store. Still, Virginia wasn't making enough money, so she began earning extra income by tutoring chemistry for other students.

At the end of her junior year, Virginia attended a summer program in research. That's when she found out that grad school was a possibility since it was government funded. As a young, single mother, Virginia earned her PhD, partly because education had always been important to her but also because she didn't know what she wanted to do at that time, nor could she afford anything else. Earning her degree also meant that she had to teach, affording her the opportunity to have a regular salary while she went to school.

"When I was teaching, I would take my daughter with me and she would quietly sit in the back of the class with her snacks," Virginia remembers. "At that point I was in grad school and working as a teacher's assistant. I never really had the undergrad, student life experience because I was trying to raise a young child while also going to class. I couldn't just go and hang out with friends like other students."

But not all was for nothing. Throughout the challenges of raising a child alone while striving to complete her education, Virginia has succeeded in obtaining her bachelor's degree in chemistry and a PhD in biochemistry, and she's now doing postdoctoral work to help diversify her field of studies.

In many ways, and like many young, single mothers, Virginia acknowledges that having a child at a young age helped her grow up. "My daughter has taught me a lot. She's in high school now and has done well for herself. She's athletic. She's a little shy and quiet. She's also very funny and charismatic. She loves animals, and she's free-spirited."

When asked what advice she would give to other young

girls who find themselves in a similar situation, Virginia had this to say: "I think it's important to know that your life isn't over just because you get pregnant. Mistakes that are made do not define who you are or what your story is going to look like. Other people look at us and think, "How are they going to do it? How are they going to raise a child?" I am in no way advocating for teenage pregnancy, but I don't think that even an older adult or married couple is ever really ready for the demands that having a child brings into your life. You can't fully prepare yourself to have a child because you never know what type of child you're going to have or what obstacles are going to come your way. No one is ever completely ready. But I think having a child can force you to think outside of yourself as you gain new strength. Strength that you never knew you had."

Virginia's story is one of hope, one that demonstrates that you can still have a dream and you can still be whatever you want to be as long as you're willing to remember who you are. The ability to look forward and not dwell on the challenges is truly a strength. Virginia went from being a high school student with an unplanned pregnancy to living a life filled with challenges. And yet she never let go of what was important to her: an education.

Along with her earned degrees, today she's also extremely proud of the relationship she has with her daughter. Life truly does continue, regardless of our circumstances. It's up to us to look at the rainbow regardless of the rain. And as super-women, we learn to wear our capes with pride and dignity.

NINE

THE MANY PHASES OF PARENTING

IF YOU'RE LOOKING FOR INFORMATION on the different stages that babies and children go through, you won't have to look hard. Oodles of articles and books are written about this. As a first-time mom, these serve as great guidelines to what you can expect in terms of development and behavior. And if you're on your second or third child, a reminder is always appreciated. While every kid is different, developing to the beat of her own temper tantrums and growing spurts, there are fixed stages that we can't avoid. Everything from teething to the terrible twos and beyond is always best dealt with when we're given a little bit of a heads-up. Not only does it let us know that we're not the only ones wondering why our children are behaving like erratic aliens; it also reassures us when we hear "that" question screaming in our brains. You're wondering, "What question?" But really, you already know what I'm talking about. In fact, as soon as I share it with you, you'll be like, "Ah, yes. *That* question."

Scenario: You look over toward your toddler, who is quietly watching YouTube videos on your phone, and two conflicting emotions meet in the center of your chest like the street gangs in *West Side Story*. The first emotion is a sense of reassurance. Your child is safe and content, and you realize that this is your chance to clean up the kitchen and perhaps throw in a load of laundry. Or perhaps just go pee by yourself. The second emotion is a little more vicious. It's a looming feeling of darkness also known as . . . you guessed it: guilt. As you observe your child's face, eyes mesmerized by the screen of your phone, you can practically hear his brain cells sizzling into a dormant, apathetic state. You look out the window, your thoughts lean toward the sunny day, and you realize that really, your child should be playing outside instead of on your phone.

"Okay, screen time is over," you say as you reach for your phone. "Let's go play outside."

And that's when it happens. Within a nanosecond, your child has thrown himself on the floor with a thump, and the walls of your home are resonating with a wailing "Noooooooooo." You're certain that random people walking two cities over can hear this, and you can even hear their silent head nods as they judge you as a parent. That's when your brain starts screaming.

What am I doing wrong?

Yup. That's the question. And the answer to that is a simple "nothing." You're not doing anything wrong. Your child's second birthday is in a few weeks, and this behavior is called the "terrible twos." You're reminded of this because you read an entire chapter about this developmental stage in that book you bought when you first became pregnant. You've also read about the terrible twos in about thirteen online articles. The question—*that* question—stops screaming and is replaced with a quiet knowing. "This is 'normal' behavior," you say to yourself. Suddenly the street gang versions of reassurance and guilt nod as they pass each other by. There will be no inner conflict today. And you walk out of the room. (You've also read that sometimes the best way to deal with a temper tantrum is to ignore it until the sweet disposition that also resides inside your child returns to the surface.)

Speaking from experience, it is possible to take the "ignore" tactic a little too far. For example, when my kids were nearing their second birthdays, I did my best to convince them that they were going to be turning seven years old. Yup, that is correct. We'd be approaching a birthday and while getting dressed in the morning, I would coo, "Is someone going to be *seven* soon?" Or during bath time in the evenings, "Who's the big girl that's turning *seven* tomorrow?"

At the time, I believed that the best way to deal with the terrible twos was to avoid them altogether. I did this with all four of my kids. And since two were born in the 1980s and two in the 1990s, I have come to the conclusion that regardless of the different decades and therefore trends, my strategy of trying to skip over the terrible twos was completely futile. The hardcore truth is that the terrible twos are a real thing. It may be hard to imagine, but I've also concluded that even the many generations of the royal family can go to the mall or a friend's house for supper and get to publicly experience their toddler's meltdown. (Or perhaps they just don't bring their children out into the public eye until they're in their late thirties. It's hard to tell.) I don't actually follow the royal family. I'm just trying to demonstrate that the terrible twos happen to *everyone*. And to help you with that, I'd like to point out that wine is a great strategy. (Also speaking from experience.)

That said, information on the varying phases of ourselves—as parents—is a little harder to find. But really, parenting is just another phase in the journey of life. And since a journey usually begins with an unassuming first step in a specific direction, parenting is more of an awakening. It's like the sudden realization that you're sitting in the middle of a mountain-sized pile of dirty laundry. And while being a mom (or dad, if that's your thing) may seem like one long journey that lasts the rest of your life, it can actually be broken down into phases. To be more precise, five phases. I don't know about you, but I like breaking things down into bite-sized chunks, because it helps with that sense of feeling overwhelmed that often seizes our days.

PHASE 1: OBSERVING

This phase actually begins way before you become a parent and often long before your body has even reached puberty. I believe this is because the Creator of humans—call it God, Source, Mother Nature, or an alien scientist that created us, using planet Earth as a petri dish—was afraid of us dying out and therefore included the inherent need to procreate in our DNA. When you think about it, it's a good plan and may have been inspired by the photocopying machine. But that's just a theory.

This first phase is a phase of noticing. Noticing that babies are cute. Noticing that you like playing with them even more than you like watching TV. There are no official stats on this, but I'm going to go ahead and say that this is perhaps because we feel an affinity to babies, having recently been that age ourselves.

Case in point: your mother's friend comes over with her six-month-old baby, and all you want to do is hold it, feed it, take it into your bedroom and set it up on your bed next to your dolls and serve it tea.

The Observing phase is more emotional connection than it is physical. It preps us into believing that having babies, no matter where our young minds think they come from (the cabbage patch, FedEx delivery, an adult saying, "Look what I found in the dryer!"), is a natural evolution of adulting. And like all phases, it's a stepping-stone to the awakening of your body that will take place years into the future. Why the early start? It's one part conditioning, one part fear—although not "our" fear but the fear of the alien creator that is afraid of us dying out. (Clearly "something" perceives us as slow learners, given that this phase begins at such a young age, giving us plenty of time to prepare.)

PHASE 2: WANTING

At some point in our hormonal coming of age, your glands explode, and suddenly your body is filled with a glittery substance. This glittery substance, also known as hormones, dazzles and changes your body while connecting your emotions to eleven million invisible detonators. You no longer recognize yourself during this phase, but the real victims here are usually your own parents.

Whereas phase 1 takes place within your emotions, this second phase is an awakening of the body. Specific body parts that were once solely associated with plumbing are now connected to an electrical force field. Your body changes, and so does your bedroom, whose walls you've plastered with posters of all your celebrity crushes. Suddenly your focus is divided in two as your attention is either on the posters or on the giant mirror you've insisted you now need in your room.

Then you meet a boy (or a girl), and all of a sudden, this dazzling substance causes your body to tingle, and you begin to imagine yourself with a baby of your very own—although this new attraction to other humans is not the trigger to your looming parental role. The trigger is the melding of hormones and changing bodies that are finally catching up to what happened within your emotions during the Observing phase. Note that the Wanting phase is subtle and could last years. Or simply hours. It's a case-by-case.

PHASE 3: PREGNANCY

Realizing that another human is growing inside of you is hardly ever like how they show it in the movies. No one walks up to you and says, "OMG! You are glowing, girl! You must be pregnant!" Instead, it goes something like this: You're meeting friends for breakfast and within seven seconds of being seated, your soul is attacked by the overwhelming aroma of everything. You quickly push your friend out of the booth to make a quick getaway to the bathroom so that you can wrench out a lot of nothing. Head down and embarrassed, you make your way back to your friends. No one says anything, because no one knows yet if this is a "good thing" or not.

Once the word is out, the Pregnancy phase is filled with wonder, curiosity, and preparation. In fact, no one is consumed by any one topic more than a pregnant woman. No matter where you are, other pregnant women seem to be everywhere. And do you know what else seems to be everywhere? Babies and children. You'll be at a local family restaurant, and more than see, you will *hear* all the babies around you. They're crying, whining, but this doesn't affect you at all, because you *know* that your baby is going to be the noncrying, nonwhining type. How do you know this? Because you're going to be the perfect parent with the perfect baby. Of course, you are!

The best part of the Pregnancy phase is the surprise baby shower. It's also the *unbest* part. First of all, it's hardly ever a surprise, because during the weeks leading up to the shower, you keep catching your significant other on the phone with your best friend, and now you're wondering if they're having an affair. Second, this "party" is supposed to be for you, and yet you're the only one who can't drink the white sangria. But it's not all bad. You get to unwrap a bunch of presents for your impending bundle of joy, which will keep you busy for the remainder of your pregnancy as you wash, fold, and unfold, and refold, and unfold, and refold until the special day arrives.

PHASE 4: LABOR

The day has finally arrived. And even though you've spent much of the last forty weeks asking everyone you know (and some you don't know) about contractions and what they feel like, you suddenly understand everyone's evasive behavior to what you thought was a simple question. *Because it feels like a freaking blender is in your uterus.* The good news is that while giving birth to babies is something women have been doing since way before the invention of Sudoku on our cell phones, the experience comes with its own set of hormones that make us *forget* about the pain. This is why we go on to have more babies. (Nice play, Creator of humans. Nice play.)

After what feels like a lifetime of walking around with what feels like a bowling ball pushing down on your bladder, and in just a few long hours, you are finally going to get to put a face to that bowling ball. This is an exciting day. It's what the focus of your life has been all about since you were about six years old, when your mother's friend came over with her baby and you got to bring it in your room and serve it tea.

PHASE 5: THE REST OF YOUR LIFE

Being a parent is perhaps the most important job you'll ever do. That said, rest assured that you will screw up. You'll yell when the windows are open and never look your neighbors straight in the eyes again. You'll resent your kids for the amount of homework they bring home from school. (Have I mentioned this already? Yes, I have. But it's worth repeating, because repeating is reminding, and reminding is remembering, and remembering is knowing that it's not just you.) And you'll order so many pizzas that the girl at the takeout counter will put your order through as soon as she sees your number on the call display. You'll believe that every other parent is doing a better job than you, and you'll wonder if you'll ever get to enjoy another hangover.

Then one day you'll realize that your aptitude for parenthood isn't the problem. The problem is in your ability to pour a sticky layer of self-doubt into everything you do. And then you'll be tucking in your kids one night, and little arms will reach around your neck and whisper, "I yuv you, Mommy," and you'll realize that being a parent is the best unassuming step you've ever taken and that you never want this journey to end. (Although you may still secretly wish for help with the laundry.)

TEN

DATING AS A SINGLE MOM; OR, HOW I MAY HAVE MISTAKEN A FEW LIFE LESSONS FOR SOUL MATES

A FUNNY THING HAPPENS WHEN you write about your own experiences. You get to go back in time and confront a younger, more naive version of yourself. And as I reflect back, I'm realizing that at one time, I was in possession of a superpower. Not the kind that Marvel or DC heroes have, like flying or the ability to fight off evil villains. (Unless you count "guilt" as an evil villain. Then yeah, totally.) Instead, it's a superhuman capacity to make my future self cringe at some of the stuff I've done. That future self is me today. Thankfully, younger me wasn't aware of this ability, because I most certainly would have abused my powers. (You think putting tennis socks in my bra was good? Wait until you see what I do next!)

As far as superpowers go, I was way too young to have been bestowed with such a tremendous ability. I suppose that if I wasn't being so hard on myself, I'd call it a rite of passage.

It is my hope that by sharing my experiences, and especially my younger self's mind-set, you will choose to take another path and avoid the rite of passage completely.

Repeat after me: *The rite of passage SUCKS.*

Once upon a very long time ago, when my scanty possessions boasted a youthful glow that clashed against the rough edges of my inexperience in the ways of love, I suffered from a heart that was both full and empty. The full side of my heart enjoyed a ritual of Friday night movies with two giggly little girls, picnics on the living room floor, and milk in our wineglasses. These Friday night rituals have turned into a treasure box of the fondest memories for my girls and me. Unfortunately, I wasn't aware of this at the time.

Meanwhile, the empty side of my heart ached for adult conversations, long gazes into desiring eyes, and actual wine in those damn wineglasses. Somehow, the empty side of my heart had decided that hugs from tiny, trusting arms and a fridge door that swelled with misspelled Crayola love notes weren't enough. To this day, it amazes me at how much power I was able to give to my loneliness. Possibly this was another superpower that I was way too young to have been in charge of.

It was during this time that the empty side of my heart took over my intentions with such brute force that I was vaguely aware of its secret mission: to find a man. Not just any man but a man who I could call my very own. A man to share my life with. The good. The bad. And yes, the ugly. Although back then, I worked very hard at making the ugly as pretty as possible, as I'll explain in a minute or two.

Despite my own emotional handicaps, insecurities, and delusions about the true meaning of love and her many faces, I was going for a very specific kind. I was going for "unconditional love." But if I'm going to be honest with myself, and therefore with you, I have to admit: I had no idea what unconditional love meant. My ability to spell the term correctly—*U-n-c-o-n-d-i-t-i-o-n-a-l L-o-v-e*—was in direct conflict with my understanding of its meaning. Not with my children but in the ways of romantic love. (Why am I even explaining that?)

I know this because while I wanted to share everything, I also had delusions of perfection. At the time, I believed that working at a relationship was about hiding as much of my ugly as possible. I was shallow that way. I know this now. But back then, that's exactly what I wanted: a relationship that revealed no ugly. Just blissful and forever-after happiness. I blame this delusion on Hollywood movies, specifically romantic comedies. (Damn you, romantic comedies!)

I call the empty side of my heart's mission "secret" because I also realize now that I wasn't even fully aware of just how lonely I was. Or that the loneliness that seemed to consume me was actually a *choice*. Instead of seeing my life for what it was, a busy attempt at doing my best with the most important people in my life (my children), I *chose* to focus my attention on the hole where a husband or, at the very least, a boyfriend should have been.

The other reason I call the empty side of my heart's mission "secret" is because the outside world—a small circle of coworkers, day care teachers, and varied bus drivers who chauffeured my life between said coworkers and day care teachers—had no clue of my heart's longings. I'm certain of this, because in those days, I worked very hard at conveying my world as one of determined self-sufficiency. I was Single Mom. I knew how to make a gazillion different meals out of a pound of hamburger meat. I was invincible. I wore my Single Mom label like Superman wears his cape. Boy, was I dumb. (Not a question.)

I, along with my well-concealed disappointment with life, had taken on the world. And we—my disappointment and I, as directed by the empty side of my heart—were on a mission to fix this. (You can't see me, but I'm rolling my eyes right now.)

If I can step back into the present, just for a moment,

there's a lot to be said about growing older and finding your wisdom. People have been talking about the fountain of youth since forever, and while the loss of a youthful glow and beginnings of graying roots may be the regret of anyone with a mirror, ignorance and naïveté replaced by wrinkles and knowingness is actually an achievement. And despite our fascination with and glorification of youth, age attained with grace is quite beautiful. I can say this now that I've already celebrated the twenty-first anniversary of my thirtieth birthday. (You see, younger me, I can make you cringe too!)

Why am I rambling about the differences between youth and age? Because as I write this, a memory stands out in my mind like a signpost. This memory, although of something seemingly insignificant at the time, is of passing words said to me by a boss when I was in my early twenties.

"You should probably try less hard at appearing so independent," he'd said to me. At the time, I thought it was a random statement. I now realize that he most probably saw right through me. I was the younger. He was the wiser. And as the wiser, he obviously saw right through my mantra back then, which was pretty much "I can change my own damn lightbulbs!"

The truth is that I desperately wanted someone whom I could call "my boyfriend." A strong shoulder to lean on. A soft voice to talk to at night after my girls had gone to bed. And of course, someone to change my lightbulbs. And by that, I really do mean my lightbulbs; there's no hidden sexual meaning here. I was tired. Tired of being responsible for every damn thing. In case you need reminding, single mothers have a special kind of relationship with "tired."

In my defense (or possibly warped understanding of affections), appearing un-needy was the first test of true love. If a man could break through my thin layer of ice-cold independence just long enough to make an impression on me (a minute or two was really all it would take), then maybe—just maybe—he would be worthy of my trust. Or something.

It was during these dark ages, also known as "before the internet became a household necessity," that I discovered online dating.

But how, you ask, could online dating have existed without the internet?

Well, if you're young enough to ask the question, let me assure you that there is a logical explanation. And if you're old enough to know the answer, please bear with me as I explain such barbaric times.

Allow me to take you through a time capsule, to a time before sagging jeans and intentionally revealed butt cracks. It was the early 1990s—an era when lace adorned everything from T-shirts to hair clips, radio stations played Madonna's "Vogue" fifty-seven times a day, and jeans were worn at belly button height. *gasp* *I know.*

This era's archaic version of online dating comprised one simple device: the telephone. And by telephone, I mean the kind that you couldn't throw in your purse on your way to the gym, because for it to work, it needed to be attached to your apartment with . . . wait for it . . . *wires and stuff.* Remember, this was a time when words like *text* and *ping* had yet to be converted into verbs, *blue* and *tooth* were rarely used in the same sentence, and people didn't feel the need to share with the world what they were eating for supper. It just wasn't possible.

It was through this device—the nonmobile telephone—that the empty side of my heart was determined to meet the man of my dreams. Of course, with my history of getting involved with unreliable, feral men, I was vaguely aware that my biggest challenge would be to find the right balance between raising my standards from past mistakes and keeping an open mind to, well, new mistakes.

While I wasn't naive enough to believe that I would meet a movie star or the real Prince Charming (although I secretly did wish for this), I did have a short list of requirements. The top of my list? He had to be handsome. Oh, and taller than me. Also fun, know how to fix things, love kids (not all kids, but mine), have a job, have a car, have a sense of humor, know how to cook, like the countryside, and enjoy movies, music, reading, and exercising.

To today's version of myself, this list sounds like half the global population of men after a few drinks. As a list, it's both vague and precise. Also unrealistic, since real connections have nothing to do with someone's height or his ability in the kitchen. I should know. My kitchen hates me.

While turning to telephone dating seemed—*eh ehm*— beneath me, no one I knew fit my description of the ideal man, so like a slave chained to the empty side of my heart, I complied with its mission. Besides, my expectations were broken. What could I possibly have to lose? Nothing. I was driven by both hope and boredom after I'd put my kids to bed.

So, one evening, I was sitting on the couch with some old friends, namely, hope and courage, both the result of drinking half a bottle of grocery store wine. It was because of the encouragement from these friends that I decided to create a "profile" on this telephone dating system thingy. Lucky for me, the service was free for women. Anyone who has ever gone through the experience of raising kids alone knows that it's an awful feeling when your expenses don't cooperate with your budget. That said, spending money on a quest to find a man is probably a luxury.

"My name is Amanda. I'm twenty-five. Have brown hair and eyes, and I enjoy long walks and movies."

Hmm. Too short.

"My name is . . . Vanessa, yes, Vanessa. And I love to go out for dinner. Um, not that I'm overweight. 'Cuz I'm not . . ."

ERASE. ERASE. ERASE.

"Hi. I'm interested in meeting interesting people who like to do . . . stuff . . ."

Who like to do stuff? What am I? A Neanderthal?

Getting my profile down just right (translation: to a point where I didn't sound stupid or desperate even to myself) took the entire evening and the second half of that bottle of wine. By that time, courage had already left the room, and I was left with hope. Also curiosity, not knowing what I was getting myself into.

Finally, with my profile recorded, saved, and "out there" for the world of men to fall in love with (I imagined), it was time to listen to the profiles of men in my selected category: long-term relationships. New to the phone-dating scene, my first reaction was gluttonous astonishment: "Wow! A man catalog!"

There were tall voices, short voices, confident voices, intelligent voices, not-so-smart voices, and even handsome voices. I definitely had stumbled onto something great. (I thought.) My second reaction, as expressed to my mother the very next day, was pleasant surprise.

"I'm amazed at how much I can tell about these men from their profiles. It's like I *know them* just from listening to their voices talk about themselves."

As I remember, my mother's response was silence. Although in hindsight, her raised eyebrow spoke a wise tale of undeniable doubt. Also judgment. But I didn't care. As far as I was concerned, I had stumbled onto a gold mine. A *man* gold mine. Besides, what could my mom possibly know about the modern invention of telephone dating?

Young, naive, and somewhat desperate to find love, I had a lot to learn during my early experiences with telephone dating. For instance, it didn't take me long to notice how easy it was to connect with a handsome voice as I listened to him tell me about his blue eyes and love for Italian food. It was the connecting-in-person part that was the problem. It took a while for me to realize that what I was really connecting with over the phone was my own expectations. This is because love, as they say, takes time to grow from a spark into something real. And real love doesn't flourish just because you're willing it to happen over a cup of coffee. Obviously. (Although perhaps not yet obvious to me at that time.)

Speaking of coffee, those early dates also taught me that first encounters should always be of the closest coffee shop kind. While you may be expecting to meet Mr. Wonderful (because that's how he sounds on the phone), eleven times out of eight, the connection you made with him on the phone will be awkward and disappointing in person.

MY FIRST ENCOUNTER OF THE DISAPPOINTING KIND

If you know me in real life, you know that I have the memory of a peanut. Don't ask me what I had for dinner last night, and especially don't ask me where I put my glasses. But when it comes to "firsts," I'm like an elephant: I remember every last detail. And so you'll understand why my very first "date" through the telephone dating service is forever etched in a squeaky, web-filled corner of my mind. And as I blow the many decades of dust from this corner, what I remember most about this "first" is how I believed—*truly believed*—that this was going to be "the one" for me. The one true love. Spoiler alert: boy, was I wrong.

His name was Robert, and as you may already suspect, Robert was not "the one." In fact, the number *one* didn't bother to make an appearance in anything to do with Robert. We had spoken on the phone exactly three times before agreeing to meet in person. The date of our first meeting was scheduled for two days later. Then on said date of our meeting, Robert left me a message on the dating line telling me that he had to reschedule. Finally, eight days later, which, according to my math, is a long freaking time when you're eager to meet Mr. Right, we met.

As I was getting ready for our breakfast date, my vision of the future was consumed with thoughts about Robert and our life together. I had already conjured up exactly what he looked like. Tall, dark, and, yes, handsome. The scenarios I played in my mind of how we were going to live forever happily ever after—the care I took in planning exactly how I was going to make room for him in my closet (well, not him exactly, but his clothes)—was nothing if inaccurate.

A little overanxious (and overdressed for breakfast), I arrived at the restaurant only to find that my knight in shining armor was a little on the short side. And by "a little," I mean, what's the official height to classify someone as a little person? Note that I have nothing against little people. Or even short people. My own children were short at one time. But Robert really should have mentioned this to me before we met. I mean, did he think I wouldn't notice? While I was driven by my own expectations of perfection (and list of requirements that made up my ideal man), he was delusional if he thought I could overlook his neglect to mention his size. Not because of his size, but because I saw this as untruthful.

Next!

A LESSON IN THE ART OF LISTENING

Listening is always important, but while you're still at the phone stage of online dating, I got to realize that listening is even more important. It didn't take long for me to get this lesson down pat. And I don't just mean listening to the words but listening to everything. Listening to what's not being said. Or listening to other sounds. This I learned from someone we'll call "Jimmy." (Since he wasn't a "first" on any level, I don't remember his name.)

On the phone, Jimmy was faultless. He was polite, funny, smart—I really enjoyed speaking with him. Confession: after our relationship ended, which, coincidentally (or not), took place at the precise moment of our first in-person date, I actually missed him. Or at least, missed our phone time. In hindsight, I did notice during our telephone conversations that whenever he said a word containing the letter s *(sweet, sophisticated, sure),* my ear picked up on a faint whistling sound that I chose to ignore. Of course, I didn't put two and two together until we met in person. The reason? Jimmy was missing a few teeth. And by a few, I mean the front row. The *entire* front row. Again, I have nothing against missing teeth. My own children were born without them.

Failed expectations and fallen heart, Jimmy wasn't the one for me either.

Of course, not all of my telephone dating encounters ended after the first meeting. Some turned into actual boyfriends. Although now that I'm older and wiser (mostly older, slightly wiser), I can say with a hundred percent certainty that in my recklessness to find true love, I may have mistaken a few life lessons for soul mates. One in particular comes to mind. We'll call this life lesson "Brandon."

Brandon was a boyfriend with whom I spent a devoted and tormented eight months.

White lies are common. I get that. But with Brandon, I learned that white lies come in a rainbow of shades. Like when someone asks you to pick up milk on your way home from work and instead of stopping, you practice the fine art of saying "Oh, crap. I forgot!" because you're just too damn tired to haul your ass into a grocery store. This is a white lie that falls in the category of the most common shade of white lies. Common, because no one gets hurt, and how could anyone possibly prove otherwise?

Or when someone compliments you because you look particularly pretty that day and you respond with a shrug of nonchalance because you don't want anyone to know just how long it took to get your hair just so. Or that back in your apartment, your bedroom looks like a home invasion because before heading out, you spent two hours tearing through your closet for the perfect outfit. I'm sure you recognize this as another common shade of white lie. Again, no one gets hurt, and no one can disprove your shrug of indifference.

And then there's Brandon. A compulsive liar, Brandon, also known as that time when life was trying to teach me the importance of listening to my own inner voice, turned out to be a complete setback in my sense of self-worth and growth as a twentysomething young woman. Not only did he lie about *everything* but he also abused my emotions to the point where I lost all ability to trust my own judgment. Looking back, eight months should have been eight minutes, had I been paying attention. But since I was instead focused on a desperate determination to fill the empty side of my heart, I not only lost time during those eight months; I also lost myself.

The recovery period after Brandon was both swift and long. Swift, because since I was really only in love with the idea of love, and not with Brandon himself, it didn't take that much time for my disappointed heart to mend. A few weeks at the most. Long, because disappointment can bruise a person's self-esteem in ways that change her entire perspective—on both how she sees herself and how she experiences the world. Brandon's effect on my sense of self-worth was transformed into a tattoo on my soul. Unfortunately, this took years to remove.

FAST-FORWARD TO TODAY

Looking back, I realize that my biggest lesson of all goes even deeper than anything I could have learned from a telephone dating service. In truth, I was putting too much emphasis on the empty side of my heart, when really, the full side had enough power on its own to overflow and fill up my entire universe. I'm sure you've heard this before: *happiness is an inside job.*

Yet I was so intent on finding love that I forgot who I was and spent way too much time seeking out the right person to whom I could give away my power—my power to *choose* happiness instead of loneliness. Looking back, what I really should have been focusing on was the side of my heart that was already full. That's where the real power resides. Always. And it is something that we all possess. It's the power of choice—the power to choose what we focus on. I didn't realize this at the time, but by focusing on my loneliness, I was actually feeding it.

If I could go back in time, I would celebrate the rituals that I shared with my kids even more often than just once a week. The Friday night movies on the VCR and picnics on the living room floor—and as I filled their wineglasses with milk, I would have put actual wine in mine, instead of waiting to toast life with the man of my demented dreams.

If I could go back in time, there's one specific thing I would change: my focus. I didn't "need" a man in my life. What I should have been focusing on was my kids and the short time I would have with them. At the time, I thought they would stay little and mine forever. The truth is that they grow up fast. Too fast. And while I love the memories, I miss those days. I truly do.

A CHAT WITH
ADRIENNE
DELAWARE, UNITED STATES

Thoughts on complacency and change

YOU'VE HEARD IT BEFORE: "SOMETIMES we are our own worst critics." We do all the right things, follow our own sense of morals and principles for how we believe we should raise our children. We walk down a long, solitary path carrying a laundry basket filled with muffled questions. The load on our shoulders is as heavy as a brick house. The support we crave is silent yet screams at us from the depths of a hollow sense of inadequacy. A need to prevail seems to have lost its luster as shadows of our internal demons look upon us with judgment. Our exhaustion exhausts us.

Mostly, our demons comprise past choices and decisions. We judge them. They judge us. Adrienne is the mother of five boys. At the time of this writing, her eldest is twenty-seven, her youngest is twelve. The bookends of a nineteen-, eighteen-, and fourteen-year-old. The four youngest of her children were fathered by a man with an addiction: crack cocaine.

Adrienne met her husband in 1997. As often happens,

she was fully immerged in the relationship by the time she realized that her husband lived with a secret dependence that had already taken over his life. "He never contributed financially to the household," Adrienne admits. "He was in jail more than he was at home." It's a story we often hear: of a man with an addiction who steals from his own family to support his habit.

In 2006, four children and nine years later, Adrienne finally left her husband for the last time. She was crying on the couch after he had just raped her when she heard exactly what she needed to hear in that moment in time. Although the TV had been on for probably over an hour, voices mumbling in the background, her attention was suddenly caught by a piercing message: "Stop being complacent. Get up and do something!" For Adrienne, the voice coming from the television was speaking directly to her.

"That's exactly what I needed to hear," she says. "That's when change started. I got showered, got dressed, and I went to the family court building for my divorce papers."

Why did it take Adrienne so long to leave a horrid situation? This question, although easy to ask, is filled with contradictions. We get married and we're told that it is "for better or worse." Family members tell us to leave, while society, including the church, tells us that we must "stick by our man." Reminders are everywhere that drug addiction is a disease. The struggle—should I stay, or should I go?—is real. Both feel right; both feel wrong. Doing the right thing is never part of the question. We want to do the right thing for everyone—our children, our husbands. Will they change? Can they change? Am I giving up on him too soon? Is there hope? Until finally something breaks. It's either our spirit or our man's hold on us. His hold on our emotions and our conscience. The hope is that the hold is never on our spirit.

But as anyone who has ever been left holding the bag of consequences knows, for Adrienne, if life "with" her husband was difficult, the solitary road of raising her boys as a single mother was filled with obstacles and challenges. Her eldest son, from a previous relationship, was seven years old when Adrienne met her husband. And with the understanding of a child, he couldn't get past the abuse that he'd witnessed. To this day, there's a great divide between the two sets of half-brothers. Meanwhile, the younger boys are left with a degree of resentment toward their father that has the power to haunt them for years to come.

Yet life for this single mother continues. Left alone to raise her boys since she was thirty-five years old, Adrienne has managed to do her best by her boys by living up to her standards as a parent. Not an easy feat, especially in today's world, where even the best of parents rely on video games as babysitters. Not Adrienne, though. It seems her values and integrity leave no room for her to take the easy way out.

"I never gave my kids video games. Ever," Adrienne says after admitting that her boys suffer from attention-deficit hyperactivity disorder (ADHD). "I was so afraid that they were going to be the worst-case scenario."

Athletic by nature, Adrienne's boys have been involved in sports since they were two years old. Basketball, football, soccer, baseball—although a great way to keep active boys busy and out of trouble, involving them in organized sports comes at a high price indeed, in terms of both time and money. But Adrienne believed that the benefits would also fill a void in her boys' lives.

"I had all these visions," says Adrienne. "I thought, 'Yes. This is what you need to do. Get them involved in sports. Coaches are great. They'll help them out. They'll teach them the man stuff that I can't. They'll talk to them about girls.'"

Looking back, Adrienne knows that her parenting style was based on what she knew at the time. And while she still beats herself up with feelings of guilt (how would life have turned out had she chosen another man to father her children?), she also did some things very right. With memories lingering from her childhood when she missed her own mother, who worked during suppertime, Adrienne made the decision from day one that she would always be home for supper and that they would always eat at the table as a family.

"Did this benefit my children?" she asks out loud. "I may not know until they're in their forties."

As any working, single mother knows, being home and preparing meals day in and day out is not an easy task. Adrienne works full time as an adolescent treatment services coordinator with the Division of Prevention and Behavioral Health, where she coordinates mental health and substance abuse services for children and their families. It may go without saying, but I'll mention it anyway—her experience with her husband and his crack addiction and abuse has given her the added advantage where she understands the people with whom she comes into contact on a level that sometimes cannot be explained. "I look at them sometimes and I think, 'Wow! You are me. I was you!'"

Throughout all of the turmoil and struggles, Adrienne has earned her associate's, bachelor's, and master's degrees. To this day, she continues to further her education, working toward her doctoral degree.

And while her spirit was not broken, she still has a hard time accepting where she's been. To this day, she continues to carry guilt like an old, tattered bag that no longer matches the life she's created for herself and her boys.

"My life has definitely been a lot of growth and a lot of experiences. Would I change some things, given the opportunity? Probably. I look at myself and who I am today, and I feel like now, with all of that trauma and all of those experiences, I would be a totally different person. I have constant reminders of the choices I've made and the things I've done wrong," she says.

But as I listened to her story, one thing was clear to me. Adrienne is a superwoman.

ELEVEN

MOM OR SUPERHERO?
BOTH ACTUALLY—
IT'S THE LITTLE THINGS

DID YOU KNOW THAT OTTERS hold hands while they sleep?

Yup, it's true. While sleeping on their backs, a mother and her pup will often hold hands so that they don't drift away from each other. From a parenting perspective, this invokes an endearing mental image, because no one wants her kid to drift away and into the mouth of potential dangers. After all, isn't our job to protect our children—their minds, bodies—while providing them with a sense of security?

Sadly, our children are not "ours" forever. Their innocence and needs crash into our lives, and with tender impact, they manage to break down our concrete exteriors and open us up to feelings we didn't even know we had. Our babies have an immediate power over us, changing us from self-centered and one-dimensional beings into perfectly ripened peaches, with hearts full of juicy love. Everything about us grows, including our capacity to feel frustration. This is why our bodies usually also get bigger after we become parents—so that we have a vessel to hold all this extra stuff. (Except patience. On most days, we can fit our patience into a bottle. Not a baby bottle but a wine bottle.)

"They grow so fast," we often hear people say. And we have no idea what they're talking about because when they say this, we're usually doing a little time-math of our own that says otherwise. Like when we're calculating how many meals we have to prepare, three times a day until they reach . . . what's the average age that our kids leave the nest these days? Is it thirty-seven?

But before that, there's the very fun and very dark tunnel of the teenage years that we must pass through and survive. Unlike the sleeping baby otter that instinctively holds its mother's hand, our teens go through organic phases of detachment as the world touches them with lessons that are theirs and theirs alone. We want to protect them—shield them—but at the same time we know that this would be unnatural. This would hinder our teenagers' growth.

Throughout the lessons and growing awareness, our kids begin to take possession of who they are. Sometimes enlightening, other times hurtful, the process takes them on a journey of self-discovery as they begin to experiment with their place within our families and the world at large. Meanwhile the parent side of us, still the same emotion-filled, juicy peach, becomes aware of our capacity to easily bruise at the slight of a tone, an attitude, periods of heartbreaking silence.

Where once we were the heroes of our children's lives, now we've become bystanders throughout their transformations. Present, yet not a part of their struggles, we stand unarmed, except for the emotional straitjacket that prevents us from intervening. From the sidelines, we watch. We watch our kids rise. We watch them fall. We hold our breaths as we watch them rise again.

When my eldest daughter was first born, I remember the words from a friend of my parents. A woman who had three children and, at the time, her youngest was around seventeen.

"The first ten years are the easiest," she had said.

My response was no response at all. I had no idea what she was talking about. We were sitting around the kitchen table, and my perfect little baby girl was sleeping in my arms, swaddled in her Tweety Bird blanket. I remember looking down at her little, round face and believing that innocence and parenting were a blissful state that lasted forever. And the funny thing is, I wasn't even drunk at the time!

My kids are grown now, and every once in a while, the small child that still resides inside their grown-ass bodies climbs out, and I get a glimpse of what it feels like to be "Mom" again. Oh, I know. I'm *always* a mom. But there's a big divide between being the mom of young kids and being the mom of teenagers and young adults. As parents, we're the same. It's our children's needs that change. And in turn, this changes who we are, not only as parents, but as individuals.

Just recently, one of my young adult children walked into the living room where I was writing and sat down on the couch. Not a word was said, and I took this as a sign. (When you're a mom, you develop a superhero ability to recognize *the signs*.)

"Yo!" (Me, using my everything-is-cool, "s'up?" voice.)

"Hey, Mom."

A gap of silence came over the room that felt like three days had just gone by. My patience was a quiet one. Then suddenly, more words. "Something happened today, and I *know* it's stupid, but it really bothered me."

"Holy *crap*! And you're coming to *me*? Wow!" (Of course, this part was said in my head.)

"Oh? What happened?" (This is what I actually said out loud.)

I'm imagining that you can imagine how hard it is to sound nonchalant when your internal dialogue is ignited by firecrackers and your imagination is like a wild horse, creating scenes in your brain faster than you can think. And then my kid's entire day rolled out like a tsunami right there in our living room. I can't share the details of the conversation, because if I did, my kid would put me up for adoption. But I can describe the *air quotes* horrible wave of events. Think big. Think roaring buildup. Think RUN FOR YOUR LIFE. Yes. *That* kind of day. We all have them. My job in all this was to make my kid see the tsunami for what it really was: *an ant splashing in a drop of water.*

And just like that, I had my job back. I felt like a mom again. A *real* mom. The great, wonderful, positive part of this story is that for the next part of the afternoon, my kid and I got to share a bag of cookies as we sat on the couch together with open hearts. The cookies (chocolate chip—store bought) were great, but more than that, we got to share words. A *real* conversation. And I got to save my kid from the little villainous happenstances that Life likes to throw on our paths once in a while. It was a good day. *Sigh.* If only it were that easy to keep them safe all the time.

TWELVE

A FEW THOUGHTS ABOUT LEADERS AND FOLLOWERS— AND BY "A FEW," I MEAN WORDS AND WORDS

WHEN MY OLDER GIRLS WERE young, around the ages of seven and four, I remember telling them that there are two kinds of people in this world: followers and leaders. And the only difference between them was their level of self-confidence. To be honest, I'm not even sure how I came up with that theory, since I, myself, had a secret relationship with confidence: on the outside, especially in front of my young daughters, I appeared to be filled with it. The truth is that I was filled with something else. Mostly bullshit. Self-confidence back then was not my friend. With visions of bullies and coercion, perhaps I was trying to prepare my girls for high school.

Since then, I've come to realize that there is a third type of person: "the individual." Neither a leader nor a follower, this type of person just gets her stuff done and doesn't give a rat's ass where she fits in with the whole hierarchical scheme of social things. Eleanor Roosevelt once said,

You have to accept whatever comes and the only import-
ant thing is that you meet it with the best you have to give.

Although there's no real evidence of this, I'm pretty sure that Mrs. Roosevelt was thinking about single moms when she said this. Have you ever noticed how certain events—no matter how insignificant they may seem at the time—stick to your memory like socks to a towel out of the dryer? Sometimes I wonder if these apparent random events don't have a deeper meaning, and that's why they stay with us.

Having reached "this age," I have a lot of memories, and there's this one memory in particular that I think about often but don't know why. My eldest daughters, about four and seven at the time (yes, the same age that I had the conversation with them about leaders and followers), were playing in the alley behind our home. I was sitting on the balcony of our third-floor apartment watching them when all of a sudden, my youngest took a hard tumble while running. No one pushed her. I think her little legs just couldn't keep up with her intentions to move forward. Naturally, she started crying (actually, it was more like wailing), and I ran down the fire escape stairs to get to her as quickly as possible. This part of the memory is vague, but I may have actually flown down those stairs.

"I hurt my knees," she said as I picked her up. I need to pause here, as the memory of her, so small and sweet, sits heavy in my chest. How I miss my kids when they were young and still mine! As I carried her up the winding staircase to clean her up, I remember her tiny arms wrapped around my neck while she sobbed into my shoulder. It was a traumatic moment. One that I remember with fondness.

In our apartment, I sat her down on the bathroom counter and gently dabbed her scraped knees with a damp wash-cloth as she continued to cry. To the neighbors, I was prob-ably pouring peroxide on her wounds. I wasn't. Nothing I said seemed to calm her down. It seemed devastation had swallowed her whole. At my wits' end, I decided to take another approach.

"It's a good thing you have those knees," I said as I focused on gently spreading Polysporin around her torn skin. "Otherwise you would have fallen on your face, and *that* would have hurt even more."

That's when the crying stopped. She looked at me for several thoughtful seconds, then pushed herself off the counter and ran back outside to continue playing with the neighborhood kids. And that was that. Why does that memory haunt me so? I can't answer why, although I do have a few theories.

At the time of this writing, this daughter is exactly thirty and a half years old. To say that I miss the little girl who used to fit in my lap is an understatement. I miss her soapy smell after bath time. I miss her little-girl voice and her long stream of questions. And yes, I even miss the whining and the crying. I miss her innocence and unwavering trust in me, even when I was tired and frustrated and yelled when I probably shouldn't have. I miss everything about that little girl. Her crabby mornings and good-night hugs. The pink bathrobe she wore at night during this particular memory and the way she would say she wasn't hungry for supper but then ask for cookies as soon as I had cleared the kitchen of all evidence that we had even had supper. I miss how she would ask "What's fow yunch?" when she was hungry regardless of the time of day, and the way she would carefully wrap a fallen tooth in tissue and place it under her pillow for the Tooth Fairy. I miss it all.

Oh, I know that our kids are our kids, whether they're two, twenty-two, or thirty-two. But now that I've gone through all the stages and can reflect, I think about how I was torn between a parental need to shelter them and a knowing that I had to encourage them to grow into independent and self-reliant individuals. Like many young parents (because I, too, was young at one time), I remember questioning myself throughout my kids' entire childhoods.

Was I too matter-of-fact that time she fell and scraped her knees? Should I have been more caring? Should I have let her go back outside, or should I have coddled her in a blankie and insisted that she stay in the house with me for the rest of the afternoon?

As parents, we hold ourselves accountable for the way our kids turn out. Yet we know that there comes a time when we need to let go. Looking back on that day, I'm glad I let her go back into the world. I'm glad she had the gumption and courage to want to continue playing with her friends. But secretly, I wish I had made a bigger deal of her scraped knees. I wish I had wrapped her up in a blanket and snuggled on the couch with her and read books with her for the rest of the day. I wish I could breathe in the soft scent of baby soap on her skin, just one more time.

Now about that third personality type. The one that doesn't give a rat's ass about where she fits in. A few years after the knee-scraping incident, I was at work (I worked for a graphic design agency at the time), and we were having a team meeting.

"We've got some tight deadlines coming up, and we're going to have to pull some late nights," our boss was telling us. The point of the meeting, I realized, was to schedule the upcoming weeks and to get us on board for overtime to make sure that deadlines were met. Being a little old school, I've always had a whatever-it-takes attitude. If the boss says "this needs to get done today," I stayed at the office until it was done. (Although not without making a few phone calls first—to my mom, or to the ex—to make sure someone could pick up my kids from school, make them supper, and stay with them until I got home. You know how it is.)

Just as my boss was putting an overtime schedule in place, one of my colleagues blurted out, "I'm not available on Tuesdays. I have yoga." The rest of the meeting went on without me, because I was dumbfounded and got stuck in the echo of her words. I was in awe. Here was this—I'll call her "girl," since she was in her early twenties at the time—who unassumingly took control of a situation and put herself first. A seemingly uneventful happenstance, yet I learned so much that day.

> Exhibit A: Me. Here I was, ready to sacrifice my evenings, which meant disrupting my kids' evening routine and possibly not getting any homework done, so that we could meet our client deadlines. If you're a single mom, you *know* what this entails. Imposing and relying on other people. A messed-up schedule. Disrupted routine. The consequences of which would have a rippling effect, potentially for days. Maybe even weeks.
>
> Exhibit B: My colleague. On the other side of the room sat an early twentyish, single woman. No dependents (she may have owned a cat), and yet she had a commitment to herself, which she respected and expressed freely. To say that I was in awe is an understatement. What did I learn that day? That we can and *should* put ourselves first. Yes, of course "getting the job done" and being "reliable" are important. But our first priority should really be ourselves. This colleague wasn't saying that she wasn't on board with the overtime and the deadlines. She was simply stating up front that she wasn't available on Tuesday evenings. Boundaries. Healthy boundaries. And confidence to set them. That, I believe, is the real difference between leaders and followers.

THIRTEEN

THE SECRET TO ADULTING; OR, FACE IT 'TIL YOU MAKE IT

CONFESSION: SOMETIMES I LOOK AT my young adult children with a slight tinge of envy. I'm guessing that I'm not the only one, because from where I stand (usually next to a mountain of laundry), our kids have it made. They have their entire lives in front of them. Their bills are minimal, if they have any at all. And their responsibilities include . . . what? Making their beds in the morning? Hardly. Emptying the dishwasher? Perhaps. At this stage in the parenting game, I've learned to pick my battles when it comes to asking for help with the household chores.

So yes. Sometimes I wish I could trade places with my young adults. This feeling was at its peak during a time when I would come home from the office and realize that I was being greeted by a sink full of dirty dishes while the humans I lived with—the ones who had been home *for hours*—were lying on the couch watching something "important" on Netflix. Oh, and then there's that lovely question that would get thrown at me before I even had a chance to unburden my shoulders from the straps of my laptop bag. I'm certain you've heard the question a few thousand times too:

"What's for supper?"

Slightly tired, but mostly overwhelmed, this question triggers a switch in me. This is when I toggle over to autopilot and simultaneously start loading the dishwasher, clearing the counter, returning phone calls, and gathering the ingredients for what I need to prepare a meal. If I'm lucky, supper will be about as elaborate as the leftovers from the night before. (Let's take a moment to acknowledge the person who invented the microwave, shall we?)

Once the phone calls are returned and I'm fully immersed in the hustle and bustle of kitchen duty, this is when my mind eases into the very fine art of daydreaming. My thoughts drift to lazy summer days—lying on a blanket in a backyard . . . reading a book . . . a soft breeze . . . butterflies . . . Hey, wait a minute! That's not a daydream. That's a memory! That's *me* lying on that blanket as a teenager. The book in my hand was actually *required* reading, because I was in summer school. And I wasn't just lethargically watching that butterfly either. I was fantasizing about being an adult and looking forward to the day when I'd get to make my own decisions. Yes, that's it. It's all coming back to me now.

I was thirteen years old, and I *couldn't wait* to live in my own apartment so that I could do whatever the hell I damn well pleased. (Although I may not have used those words specifically, because back then they weren't *allowed* in my vocabulary.) In hindsight, *what was I thinking*?

Adulting is not about freedom and making awesome decisions. In fact, quite the opposite. Being an adult comes with responsibilities and exhaustion. Being an adult is overrated and comes with feelings of underappreciation. That sense of freedom I longed for? Newsflash: it doesn't exist. Making my own decisions? *Pfft*. When you're an adult, decisions are nothing more than a renumbering of all the things. What things? You know, *the things*. The things on the to-do list. Shall I vacuum now, or after I get the towels from the dryer and fold them and put them away? Should I make spaghetti for supper, or tacos? Can I pay the electric bill and the phone bill this week, or do I have to save one for later this month? Yes, *those* things.

The dream of living on my own? Well, yes. Maybe that's something I still fantasize about on some days. Don't judge me. Here's an unspoken yet highly probable statistic: eleven out of ten parents think about running away from home . . . at least once a week.

Reality check: okay, so maybe adulting isn't what we were expecting. But being a teenager isn't all lazy summer days and chocolate either. In many ways, being a teenager and being an adult have the exact same challenges. They're both coddled in feelings of insecurity and self-consciousness. Teenager or adult, tell me you don't question yourself sometimes . . . most of the time. And here's the kicker: whether you're a teenager or an adult, they both take years of experience to master. Then, just as you start to get into the swing of one phase of life, you realize that you're entering another. No worries—I'm about to share a little secret with you.

In my many years of practice as an adult (like medical practice, but with fewer patients and more oops), I've come to realize that there's only one way to truly succeed, and it's exactly the same as getting through the teenage years. It involves following a highly developed strategy—so highly developed, in fact, that some may even call it *sophisticated*. The strategy? I call it *face it 'til you make it*. Just keep doing what you're doing and hold your head up high as you're doing it. Keep showing up. Because here's the real secret: nobody knows the rules of adulting. And those who think they do are usually just faking it. But let's not tell them that. Watching the hoity-toity screw up is one of the true pleasures of adult life. **cough** Kardashians.

Oh, wait! Let me rephrase that.

Watching the hoity-toity screw up *while sipping on a glass of wine* is one of the true pleasures of adult life. (Let's keep this our little secret.) All that to say that I guess I don't want to trade places with my teenagers after all. (At the time of this writing, they're not allowed to drink wine.)

And speaking of wine, is it happy hour yet?

One more thing before we move on. These words of wisdom do not only apply to adulting. *Face it 'til you make it* applies to *everything*. Your dreams. Your goals. Your ambitions. They just keep showing up. And on those days when you feel like nothing is working out—those days when you feel like you're spinning your wheels *for nothing* because nothing is happening? Just go to bed. You're allowed to be tired. It's okay to feel discouraged. Grab a book or a glass of wine and let your thoughts turn to something else for the evening. Tomorrow you'll wake up refreshed and ready to face it again. Just remember this: the real difference between people who succeed at their dreams and those who don't is that the ones who do went to bed feeling discouraged and woke up feeling inspired. They got back on the horse and took more steps toward their goals. The ones who never succeed—well, they went to bed discouraged and woke up thinking, "Why am I even doing this?"

They don't realize it, but that's exactly the right question to ask: why *are* you doing this (whatever "it" is to you)? If you can remember your why, you're on the right path. Unfortunately, most people respond to that question with, Is it even worth it? I'll *never* get there.

And as you can see from their attitude (and results), they're absolutely right. Don't be one of *those* people. Remember why you're working toward a goal (write it down, if you have to), and get back on your horse. Every. Single. Day.

FOURTEEN

WHEN YOUR OWN THOUGHTS ARE YOUR ENEMY

WAY BACK IN THE DISRUPTIVE corners of my mind, a thought lounges comfortably on one of those big, leather reclining chairs. It takes up a lot of space. I would love to be able to call it a "dormant" thought, but it's not. It's like when your kid pretends to be asleep, except that you know he's not sleeping because the folds in his eyelids are squeezed a little too tight. Well, that's what this thought is doing. It's squeezing itself into a blind silence while desperately trying to pass itself off as *my* thought. (The sneak!)

Why would a thought pretend to be dormant? Probably for the same reason that kids pretend to be sleeping—so that they can disturb you when you least expect it, like when you're relaxing in the bathtub at the end of a long day.

Oh, but this isn't just *my* thought. You've had it too. And while it really is quiet in its demeanor, let me assure you that it's also very powerful. So powerful that it can paralyze you. In fact, it probably has.

So, you ask, what thought are you talking about?

Patience. I'm about to tell you.

i suck.

Yup. That's the one. You may have noticed the lowercase pronoun. That's on purpose.

Despite its puffy chest and confident attitude, it's an absurd thought and one that really doesn't deserve much attention. But at the same time, it *does* deserve attention, because facing it head-on may be the only way to banish it. Like an exorcism, except with less religious chanting and more in-your-face calling out.

Perhaps the best way to evict this paralyzing thought is by dispelling a few myths. This is all stuff we—you and I—already know but may need reminding of. And sometimes we simply need to read them when we're *ready*. Ready for what, you ask? Ready for a change. Being ready can come after the eleven thousandth time that you've already read the exact same thing. Let's hope that this is that eleven thousandth *and one* time. Let's hope that the following myths sink in and change our—yours and mine—perceptions about ourselves forever. The objective? Less paralyzing and more soaring.

The truth is that we—you and I—do not suck. And yet I realize that me simply writing that—you simply reading it—doesn't help. Not one bit. If it did, I would stop writing right here and go make myself a sandwich.

We *know* we don't suck, and yet that damn thought is still there, taking up space in our minds when we should be high-fiving ourselves for our awesomeness.

(No, that was not the sound of a single clap you just heard. It was me, high-fiving myself. Go ahead. High-five yourself too. It feels kinda good. It's like forcing yourself to smile when you really don't feel like it. It moves the energy around. It distracts you from the thought lounging in your head that isn't even yours.)

So here we go. I'm about to write—you're about to read—something you've read eleven thousand times before. Cheers to eleven thousand and one. Get ready to earn your wings. Oh, wait! Before we begin, let's make a promise to each other. Raise your right hand and repeat after me:

I, _____ (Elisabeth, Charlie, Chanelle, Princess Diva Eclectic Soliloquy . . . whatever name you choose to go by; hopefully it's the last one because it sounds badass, doesn't it?), do solemnly swear to read the following myths with an open mind. I also promise not to let my eyes glaze over the words, but to *really read* them, even if I don't think that they apply to me, and let them sink in. Amen.

Yo, sistah! Virtual high-five. Ashes to ashes, thoughts to thoughts, we are now committed to one another. I'm pretty sure that in a perfect world, this means that we have each other's backs. Yay us!

Now, on to the myths . . .

MYTH 1: EVERYONE IN THE ENTIRE WORLD IS SMARTER THAN ME

We don't always think these exact words in that specific order, but much of the time, I, you, sit (sometimes stand) in a state of hushed confusion, as though everyone else has the answers to all the questions and we're just floating about in the dark, pretending to know what we're doing with arms recklessly flailing about. Think *first day of high school,* except that it's every day of your life.

Well, guess what? We're all trying to touch on something that makes sense in this world of adulting. No one is immune. No one is born with all the answers. Questions, insecurities, cautious steps forward—these belong to us all. Even the smartest person in the room doesn't have all the answers.

And here's the good news: you don't want to have all the answers. You don't even want to be the smartest person in the room. If you "think" you have all the answers, you're arrogant. Plain and simple. Also, you stop growing, and once that happens, what's the point? (That wasn't a real question.)

So, here's the deal. Everyone in the entire world is not smarter than you. Some may be stronger than you in some areas (think astronauts or mathematicians), but that's just their thang (not a typo). You have your strengths too. We all have our unique skills and talents. For example, I enjoy writing, and therefore I have let it choose me as its vocation. I have allowed writing to consume me. If you know me in real life or if we're friends online, you know that I'm a disaster in the kitchen. I'm okay with that. And my kids have learned to accept it. The point is, we're all different, with our own unique skill sets. Amen to that!

MYTH 2: EVERYONE IN THE ENTIRE WORLD IS MORE DESERVING THAN ME

Although this memory sits in one of my mind's pockets that is the size of a Montreal pothole after a long, cold winter, it pretty much sums up my place in the world.

High school. You remember those days. They were filled with sudden outbursts of pimples (usually ten minutes before an important event, like the Friday night dance) and walking cautiously through hallways as you simultaneously tried to get to your next class while praying that you wouldn't run into the bullies or mean girls or your most recent heart-throbbing crush. For that last one, you actually *did* hope to run into him, but not today. Not while your face is hosting a pimple the size of a pumpkin. *(Please, God, not today.)*

When I think back to high school, two words immediately bounce off the walls of my eardrums: Suzy Shallow.

Before I continue, I just want to point out that "Suzy" is not her real name. I'm renaming her here for two reasons. First, because although I haven't seen or heard of her in ~~over thirty years~~ a very long time, I don't feel like having my ass sued. A writer has a responsibility to protect the innocent. In this case, me. And second, *Shallow* isn't her real name either. This is my way of being a little vindictive. Don't judge me. Being a writer has to have *some* perks. And besides, a long time ago is, well, *a long time ago*. Maybe she's a nice person today. People change. People grow up. (Although perhaps not Mr. What-Was-I-Thinking. I'm pretty sure he's the same irresponsible ass *cough* never mind.)

Okay, back to our friend Suzy. Correction: Suzy *Shallow*. Except, as you're about to find out, she wasn't my friend. Not really.

Suzy was the kind of girl who had everything going for her. She wasn't just pretty. She was *beautiful*. She didn't just have nice hair. She had *perfect* hair. She wasn't just smart. She was an *honor student*. She didn't just have boobs. She was a *ten*. And her smile. She could charm her way out of gym class just as easily as she could glance over at you and give you a smirk that made you avoid the lunchroom, library, and all bathrooms until the end of the school year. That smirk said that she had you on her shitlist. The trigger for that smirk? It could be anything from a teacher commending you on an assignment in front of the entire class to you having a good hair day. (Lucky for me, I didn't spend much time on homework and never had good hair days, so I was never on Suzy's shitlist. Thank gawd!)

The only people who were really immune to Suzy's hit list were her friends—the people who made up the long train of her entourage. Although at the time, I suspected that maybe being part of Suzy's group was their way of staying safe—like home base in a game of tag, benign and untouchable.

And then one day, Suzy needed me.

A few months before that day—the day that Suzy needed me—I had a boyfriend who, unbeknownst to me, was someone who Suzy had a crush on. Long story short, I moved away, and said boyfriend and I lost touch, as often happens when you're in the throes of love and fourteen years old. Then one day, I was back in town, and who do I run into at the mall? Suzy. And she had questions. Lots and lots of questions. She asked for my phone number and promised to call me later that evening. (Because gods forbid she should ask me questions in front of her harem of friends.)

Confession: I stayed by the phone that entire evening. What could little miss popular possibly want to ask me? When I pounced on the phone for the third time that evening and it was finally her, she admitted her crush on my ex-boyfriend and proceeded to ask a gazillion questions about him. It seemed he wasn't interested in her, and she couldn't figure out why.

Do you see where I'm going with this?

This was when I realized that even Suzy, the most popular girl in school, wasn't as confident and self-assured as she let on. While the rest of us were probably all secretly wishing we could be more like Suzy, she was secretly wishing she could be more like . . . well, me. If said boy liked me and not her, what could I possibly have that she didn't? (Besides him.)

Moral of the story: again, we all have insecurities. We all think that others are more deserving than we are at times. The good news? We're all human. No one is more deserving; no one is less deserving. All you can do is be a good person and *know* that you are deserving. Thinking back, I know exactly what I had that she didn't. *I WAS A NICE PERSON, SUZY SHALLOW.*

Showing kindness and always giving your best effort, no matter what your best is at that time, automatically makes you a deserving person.

Here's the math:

GOOD, GENUINE PERSON = DESERVING

Make sense?

That said, the *i suck* belongs to us all. Some days it wins. Some days you win. Just remember that you are just as smart and just as deserving as everyone else. And that the human race isn't a race at all. We're simply beings, all at different stages of our own growth. So, go ahead. Kick that *i suck* out of the leather chair in your mind and put another new and better thought there—one that serves you instead of paralyzing you—and *soar*.

FIFTEEN

DON'T FREAK OUT, BUT CAN WE TALK ABOUT ANXIETY ATTACKS FOR A MINUTE?

IF YOU'VE NEVER HAD AN anxiety attack, let me enlighten you: it feels like your own brain is eating at you from the inside. Your thoughts are swirling, bumping into each other. Your heart is *screaming at you,* reminding you that it's there—like a boxing match is on round 27 inside your chest. And breathing feels a little like drowning in freezing cold water. It's awesome.

Still not sure what an anxiety attack feels like? Oh, well, here. Let me share a therapy session with you. Well, not a *real* therapy session, because I don't have a therapist, but if I did have a therapist, this is how it would go. We'll call my pretend therapist Barbara, because if I had a real therapist, I would want her to be called Barbara. It's a nice name for a therapist. Barbara. It sounds like it belongs to a woman who's mature and confident. Basically, everything that I'm not.

BARBARA: Hello, Mona. Have a seat. Ummm . . . or lie down. Whatever. That's okay. Get comfortable. How are you? Tell me. What's on your mind?

ME: Well . . . I'm hoping that this session will relieve the
layer of neurosis that's resting heavily on my soul and
that you'll be able to shine some warm sunlight on
it—and maybe even melt it away. I'm hopeful, if nothing else. At the moment, 7 percent hopeful; 95 percent
nothing else. I failed math. Don't judge me.

BARBARA: Interesting choice of words. Please continue.

ME: The big question: how am I doing since our last
(pretend) visit? Life is volatile. Some days I feel like I
have everything under control. And by everything, I
mostly mean my insecurities. And then I get out of
bed, and WHAM! I'm hit with the realization that I
have absolutely nothing under control. Call me a slow
learner, but I'm starting to realize that I have to work
very hard to stay one step ahead of my insecurities—*all
the time*. It's exhausting. And there's this question that
begs to be answered. The question? Why, dear Barbara,
haven't you fixed me yet? What am I even paying you
for?

Barbara writes something in her notebook.

ME: I know. I know. Questions should not *ever* have to beg
to be answered because "questions are never stupid
and they should be treated with respect" yadda, yadda,
yadda. But everyone knows that questions are *never*
treated with respect.

BARBARA: I respect your questions, Mona. Please tell me
about these insecurities.

ME: Well, it doesn't take much. I can be lying in bed at
night and hear one of my kids cough, and suddenly
my thoughts are hijacked with visions of them dying. I
spend the next hours-into-days being accosted by irra-
tional scenes that come running out from the darkest
corners of my mind to frolic. Just frolic—as though the
gods have opened the doors to Mardi Gras and it's a

big street party in my head. Sounds fun, but it's really
not.
BARBARA: Go on.
ME: And then I end up playing the role of the quiet and
appeasing host to a haunted imagination. It's draining. Actually, it's worse than draining. It's paralyzing.
It's mourning a grief that isn't based on reality and
yet insists on existing. Heavy, painful, and ridiculous.
Exactly what fighting a sumo wrestler must feel like.
BARBARA: Tell me more. What does it feel like to be
accosted by "frolicking and paralyzing thoughts"?
ME: Oh, the things I think about doing. I think about
changing careers . . . I think about selling my house
and moving into my car . . . I think about changing the
color of my hair and getting bangs. Bangs, Barbara.
BANGS! I even think about moving in with homeless
people. But even homeless people have standards. This
makes me realize that I give new meaning to pathetic.
[*I hang my head in shame.*]
BARBARA: No. This is good work, Mona. You're on the
brink of something.
ME: Oh! And then there's this other scene that goes wild
kingdom in my brain: I imagine that I'll never fall in
love and never be in a real relationship. And then I
start to blame my kitchen because it hates me and who
in their right mind would ever want to be with someone who can't even control her own kitchen?
BARBARA: Um . . . okay. Maybe we need a bathroom break.
ME: No, wait. I'm just getting started . . .
BARBARA: No. Really. I think we need a break.

*Neither of us actually gets up. Barbara reaches into her
purse and pulls out a flask, then pours its contents into
her coffee mug. Meanwhile, I'm too busy talking to let
this register.*

ME: Something else that takes all my energy is working very hard on my sense of self-worth and its effect on my life. I worry a lot about my kids getting sick. And I worry a lot about me never falling in love and having a real family. And then I remind myself that if any of this happens, it happens. So what? I'd deal with it. Meanwhile, I'm spending a lot of the present time entertaining scenarios that will probably never happen. But then I realize that that's what I'm afraid of: that they will never happen! Barbara, does any of this even make sense?

Barbara takes a gulp from her coffee mug as she doodles absentmindedly in her notepad. I thought she was taking notes. Turns out she's just doodling. It dawns on me that her coffee is spiked.

ME: I want to be in a healthy relationship. I really do. And I work very hard at that too. But then I think that maybe my "working hard at it," which may simply be me just "thinking" hard at it, is the very thing that's making me feel that my relationships aren't healthy in the first place. Some more unfoundedness for my Rolodex of confused thoughts.

BARBARA: G-on.

ME: Ummm . . . are you speaking cursive, Barbara? Never mind. I feel like in order to keep my kids healthy and find true love, I need—*need*, BARBARA—I *need* to be perfect all the time. I have to be happy and perfect Mona *all the time*. It's exhausting.

But that's just how I feel. In my kids' defense, and to everyone else I know, all is well: my kids are healthy, and my brain does not try to eat itself from the inside. I'm starting to realize that people—in general—are simple that way. And I believe with all of my logical, nonthinking sides that they're right. Perhaps. Maybe.

Also, I think I'm empathic. Barbara, what *are* you drinking anyway?

Barbara, placid, silent, possibly bored, stares incoherently at nothing, looking a little like someone who desperately wants to fall asleep. Her eyes are blank but open just a little too wide.

ME: I don't want to be the kind of person who puts all of her happiness into her relationships. So, recently I've started accepting invitations from random strangers to dinner parties. Well they're not actually random. I pick them out. Also, they're not the ones handing out invitations. I'm actually asking them if they'd like to have me over for dinner sometime. I'm also thinking about joining Toastmasters. This is to help keep me busy and to ensure that I don't make my kids and everyone else I know the center of my world.

Lucky for me, no one has any idea that I think so much. Too much. Or maybe they do and have chosen to pretend not to notice. If that's the case, they may be wiser than I give them credit for. Oh, wait! Or maybe they just don't care. I don't know. Am I overthinking this? And speaking of "thinking," I think that a little reassurance once in a while would go a long way in making me feel secure, don't you think, Barbara? In fact, I'm sure of it. Well, pretty sure. Okay. I *think* I'm sure. Maybe. I'm not sure.

And then there's the topic of *trust* . . .

BARBARA: *Snore*

ME: My biggest problem, I believe, is that I trust no one. Well, except maybe you, but I pretend-pay you so you don't count. Just the other day, I was at a client's office, and they were talking about Brad Pitt, and I said, "How could you be with someone that beautiful and feel good about that?" and this woman responded by saying, "Trust, my dear." And I thought, *trust?* Does she know I have trust issues? *Oh my God, she knows I have trust issues.* Does this mean that the entire world knows? And then the meeting started, and I lost track of my thoughts.

If I could just *trust* in my relationships. If I could just *trust* in what I have to offer and that I even *have* something to offer. If I could just *trust* that my kids are healthy and safe and that they'll *always* be healthy and safe. Then all would be right in the world. Right? I mean, if I could just trust, we wouldn't even be having this conversation.

BARBARA: *Silence*

ME: Ummmm, Barbara? Oh, and here's a surprise—I don't even trust my dogs. They would leave me in a minute if they could, the ungrateful bastards.

Holy Psychology 101, Batman! I think I've just figured out the root to my anxieties: I have trust issues! I don't even trust *life*!

Okay, so put that way, my neurosis seems almost manageable. It also almost makes me feel "normal."

Trust. All I need to do is develop trust. Easy peasy [*I say with fingers crossed—and toes and ovaries, just in case*].

So. there you go, Barbara. One longish session with you has turned into a quasi-breakthrough for me. I'm tired. Do you want to join the Mardi Gras party that's going on in my head? Looks like fun after all!

Barbara? Are you even listening to me?

Barbara?

Thoughts on finding balance

BALANCE IS SOMETHING WE ALL strive for. And as single mothers, finding balance often means that we're juggling everything at the same time, including raising our kids, running our households, and meeting the demands of work. We know this because we live it—each and every one of us, each and every day. For Donna, finding balance meant that she had a few extra items in the air to juggle. It all started when her and her former husband realized that their eldest son had a learning disability called dysgraphia. Described as affecting writing abilities, dysgraphia specifically affects the set of motor and information processing skills required for putting thoughts to paper.

"We couldn't understand why he could do long math problems yet couldn't write the answer down. That's when we started to realize that there was a problem. He was doing it all in his head, like a Rain Man sort of thing," Donna says as she reflects back to when they started noticing that their son had a yet-to-be-diagnosed challenge.

And while their son had this condition that was labeled as

a "disability," he was also an exceptional learner with a high
IQ. It seemed that his brain crossed over onto both sides of
the extraordinary. This caused frustration for Donna's son,
who was officially diagnosed with dysgraphia at age nine.
It also posed another challenge in terms of finding the right
school, one that could cater to his bright mind and unique
learning profile.

Having moved the family from Toronto, Canada, to
Newfoundland, to accept the position of creative director for
a marketing agency when her boys were four and six years
old, it was time for another move—this time to Halifax,
where the required special-needs schooling for her son's
disability would be more affordable.

That's when another challenge raised its confrontational
head. Now a single mother, Donna and her boys found themselves in a city that offered affordable schooling solutions for
her son's special needs yet no support network. They knew
no one. Donna didn't realize the burden this would be on her
children until she started noticing a change in her younger
son's behavior. As she dropped him off at school, he would
say things like "I hope you die in a car accident!"

"This was so out of character for him because he's such a
compassionate person," Donna explains. And then she found
out that the mothers of two other children from her son's
school had died in car accidents. That's when it dawned on
her that what sounded like anger was really her son express-
ing his fear. Living in a town where they knew no one and
didn't have the support of extended family, her son was afraid
of losing his mother. Feeling isolated, he felt that she was all
he had. That's when Donna also realized the importance of
having "a village."

"Eventually, we did find our village, but in the early days
I didn't realize how scary it was for my kids," Donna says
as she reflects back.

Meanwhile, Donna had another challenge to face. While
she was dealing with her eldest son's unique learning profile,

her younger son's fear and insecurities about losing her, and getting accustomed to her new role as a solo parent, Donna's mother was diagnosed with dementia. And as if that weren't enough, her mother was back in Toronto. As the family's only daughter, the responsibility of caring for her mother had fallen on Donna's shoulders. For one week every month, Donna traveled to Toronto to ensure that her mother, who had been placed in a residence, was being well taken care of.

The one good thing that Donna had going for her was that she had found a way to work from home, known today as working "remotely." This made managing her children's schedules and running her household a little easier in terms of time management. An award-winning copywriter, she had set up a virtual office and opened her own advertising agency, DoryAds.ca, which she continues to run today.

"It's a really interesting business model," Donna explains, "because it allows me and everyone I work with to have a life and own our time. Most of the women I work with also have children, and I don't really understand walls anymore. When you think about having to get to work when you're commuting, so much time is wasted with meetings and traveling and traffic. Working from home has allowed me to be there for my kids when they need me."

Of course, not everyone has the discipline to work from home. As well, many people need the daily interaction with others, which Donna found by going to her local coffee shop to work every day.

"I used to go out and make sure that when I wrote, I wrote someplace where there were a lot of people. I found it easier, creatively, to write in a room where I wasn't by myself. It's not that different, I suppose, than going into an office where you're surrounded by colleagues. It's just that you get to choose your hours."

Donna found that by going to the same coffee shop daily, she was able to build a sense of community with both the baristas and the other patrons who would also go in with their laptops to work on a regular basis.

When asked what advice she would give other single mothers looking for a way to build something for themselves, Donna had this to say: "When it comes to going out on your own and starting a business, there's an insecurity about the beginning process. How does it all work? And do we need an office and staff to look legitimate? These are really just expenditures. If there's a way to develop a business without them, my suggestion is that you'll be much better off."

As well, because you have less to manage in terms of staff and the stress of paying office-related bills on time, you get to focus more on the quality of your work. Before Donna had made up her mind to work from home, she actually did look into renting an office space. The rent would have been an overwhelming $4,500 a month.

"I felt like I didn't really have a choice. When you're raising kids, it's important to be efficient," Donna adds. "And in today's world, the internet has made it so much easier for everyone."

In conclusion, Donna has overcome many of the challenges that single mothers face plus a few additional ones—and all the while, being recognized as a top female Canadian copywriter. That's quite an accomplishment, and one that earns her a superwoman cape for sure.

But if you're thinking that all came easy for Donna and her children and that all was overcome with grace and rainbows, think again.

"My son says that when we first started, when we first moved to Halifax, all I did was yell for two years," Donna admits as she giggles at her son's interpretation. "And it's possible that he's right, because I remember being so stressed out much of the time."

I mention this because I feel that it's an important part of Donna's story. It's crucial for us to remember that while the results of our work and strife tell part of our story, the journey, the fight, and the challenges reveal who we are and how we grow. The lesson in Donna's story is that we are all capable of amazing things and that no one is immune to stress. People in general, and single mothers in particular, have been overcoming challenges since the dawn of humanity. In the moment, what matters is how we deal with our circumstances. In the end, what we remember is the strength of the relationship that we build with our children.

SIXTEEN

DEALING WITH EXES; OR, WHY I HATE ALGEBRA, AND WHY YOU'RE THE MOST IMPORTANT PART OF THE EQUATION

I'M IMAGINING THAT AFTER READING the title of this chapter, you're wondering where I'm going with this. Oh, wait! Am I being presumptuous? I hate that. Maybe you didn't even read the title. Okay, so in that case, let's go back. Let your eyes wander back up to the top of the page so that you can read the title. I mean *really* read the title, so that we're, you know, on the same page. Now go on. Read that title. I'll wait.

tap, tap, tap

No pressure. Take your time.

tap, tap, tap

Ah, back already? Okay, so at this point, you may be asking yourself, *WTF is she talking about? Exes . . . algebra?* And, putting myself in your reading chair, I would have to agree with you. Upon first glance, math and the father of your children have absolutely nothing to do with each other. Except for maybe a little subtraction within the context of your family unit. But I do solemnly swear to have a point. (Note that I typed that last sentence with my left index finger as I raised my right hand to prove my point. Which is that I really do have a point.)

Let's begin with a math problem. The entire premise behind algebra is to disguise numbers into something that they're not, namely, letters. And even though this seems a little futile (do we really care what x is?), the purpose behind this is to train our brains to see past the disguise and look at something for what it truly is. It's a crazy science, because why not just skip the mask altogether and *tell* us that $x = 4$? Or in the case of your ex, that ex = an asshole? Or perhaps not an asshole, but simply someone you've outgrown.

A REASON, A SEASON, A LIFETIME . . .

One of the hardest things to accept in life is when the person to whom you have given your all, the one you thought you'd be building a life with "until death do us part," is really not the one for you. Sometimes people just grow apart, and other times your present self wants to scream at your younger self, "*What were you thinking?*"

It's been said that you never really know a person until you live with him. I've read that to truly see a person's colors, you have to see him react in a specific situation on three separate occasions.

Scenario: He's late for a meeting and can't find his car keys.

First time: He's so discreet that you're not even aware that he's lost his keys.

Second time: You notice that he's a little flustered, and you ask him what's wrong. He tells you and you try to help him. "What's the first thing you did when

you came home yesterday?" you ask. You watch as
his eyes shift from side to side. He's thinking. And
he is calm.

Third time: He's having a meltdown. You're walking
on eggshells. This, you realize, may be the day that
you die. And all because he can't find his freaking
keys.

Or perhaps the following resonates more with your personal
experience:

Scenario: He's getting ready for a night out with the
boys.

First time: He's chill. Tells you he'll miss you before he
leaves. Spends much of his evening out texting you.

Second time: He tells you he'll miss you before he
leaves. Hours later, he texts you to tell you he's on
his way home and please order a pizza.

Third time: You notice how ridiculously excited he
is as he's getting ready to go out and realize he
wasn't that damn happy for your date night last
week. (Just an observation.) You hear the car back
out of the driveway and realize that he barely said
good-bye to you.

Here's my take on discovering a person's true colors: you
never really know a person until you break up with him.

I have a friend who claims the man she was married to
was, at the time, a great husband and father for the sixteen
years they were married. He was attentive. He was involved.
He was a good provider. Then she found out that the reason
he was all those things was because of guilt. Those long hours
at the office? He was sleeping with a colleague. Attentive and
involved? You guessed it—all driven by guilt.

Being the type of woman who believed in things like trust,
being faithful, and until-death-do-us-part, she had no choice

but to divorce him. The trust was gone, and so was their marriage. And that's when my friend's husband's "real" true colors came out. Suddenly, he went from being the love of her life to becoming the obstacle in her life. Even though he caused the divorce by cheating, now as her former husband, he did everything in his power to make her life miserable. On purpose. Translation: he was being an asshole.

My story is similar. When I finally decided to leave the father of my first two children, he decided that he was going to fight for custody, so off to the lawyer's office I went. Did I have money to spend on a lawyer? No. In fact, I can remember times when my daughters would ask me for a snack, and my response—*I don't want you to spoil your appetite for supper*—had absolutely nothing to do with the real reason. The truth was that the grocery order didn't include snacks because I was on a tight budget of essentials only.

My lawyer, an older gentleman, was actually an acquaintance of my father. I must confess, I don't even remember this lawyer's name. I simply remember him as a tall, slender man who mostly wore brown suits. Don't judge him—this was the 1980s. He didn't smile often, but he was a kind and patient man. For purposes of clarity, we'll call him Mr. Bond, for no particular reason except that Mr. Bond took me to lunch once and he had a martini, shaken, not stirred.

Mr. Bond once asked my dad, "Your daughter seems like a nice girl. How did she end up with him?" (Him being my ex and the father of my two daughters.) My dad's response? "Oh, I don't know. She was always bringing home strays." And my dad was right. Stray dogs. Feral cats. As a kid, my heart would break for stray critters, and I would bring them home. Then I grew up, and my heart belonged to stray men.

After the trips to the courthouse and sleepless nights of worrying that Mr. What-Was-I-Thinking would get my girls, he upped and left. That's right. He moved to the other side of the country, leaving his responsibilities as a father behind. I got full custody of my girls, and I even attained a judgment for child support. But since I had no idea where Mr. What-Was-I-Thinking had moved to, I received no child support. And, of course, no moral support. Zilch.

Worrying for nothing. And more than that, money spent for nothing. Money that I didn't have to begin with. In hindsight, Mr. What-Was-I-Thinking actually did us a favor. Raising my girls alone, life was not easy. But I'll tell you this: it was a hell of a lot easier without him around. So I suppose I should be grateful for that. I'm not.

Regardless, I truly believe that after he left our lives, I became a happier person. I also believe that this—my happier disposition—had a direct impact on my girls. I couldn't control how their father behaved. I couldn't "make" him be a more present dad, and I'm certain that I resented him for it. This would have had to come out in some form, whether it was being frustrated with my kids or simply being frustrated with life in general. This is where I learned that no matter what my ex was doing, not doing, doing wrong, whatever, it didn't matter, because he wasn't involved enough to matter. This is where I learned that I was the most important part of the equation. Ah, yes. We're back to math and algebra and figuring out what x is. And if x (or ex) isn't involved, it really doesn't matter. He can do, say, whatever he wants. It will impact your kids, but it won't matter as much as what *you* do and say. He can be the biggest asshole in the universe. You just can't ever admit it out loud in front of your kids.

It's unfortunate, but sometimes people don't step up to their responsibilities, and everything falls on you. I've spoken to enough single mothers from around the world to know firsthand that this happens, and it happens a lot. Not to say that women and mothers don't do the same. But that's another book and not one meant for me to write, because that hasn't been my path. The good news is that men, I've noticed, are getting more involved in raising their children. More so than when my older girls were young. It's a new generation.

Sadly, I have a very strong memory of the look on my girls' faces when I picked them up from their dad's apartment for the last time before he moved away. Little mouths turned down at the corners and sad, quiet eyes. They were heartbroken. Perhaps a piece of them broke that day. Their father wasn't perfect. He wasn't regular with visits. And he definitely didn't help out financially. But he was the proverbial "Disney dad." The random and infrequent sleepovers that they spent at his apartment were important to them. Regardless of how disappointed I was with his capacity to help out and be present, he was their father. The only man they would ever be able to call "Dad."

None of us can control how another behaves. But we can control our own actions. And trust me when I say that no matter how great or—what's the opposite of great? terrible?—he is as a father, talking shit about him will only end up hurting your kids and boomeranging back toward you. And eventually that boomerang will hit you in the stomach. Hard. Your kids will act out, and you're the one who's going to be left cleaning the mess.

And for those times when you absolutely have to see him or deal with him, there's only one way to get through it: with quiet dignity. Several years ago, I had broken up with a boyfriend whom I was going to have to see because his son and my girls were going to the same day camp, and at the end of the summer, there was a family day for which the kids and staff had prepared presentations. Now this ex-boyfriend was not the father of my children. He was just another bad decision on my part, and I knew that crossing paths with him would be uncomfortable and awkward. This is when my mother gave me some words of wisdom, and possibly the best advice for this situation and many others to boot. She said, "Stand tall, hold your head up high, and walk as though you're Marilyn Monroe walking across a stage." And that's exactly what I did. It gave me the confidence I needed to pretend I was in control. And while I was pretending, I can tell you that fake confidence is contagious. I've since used that little nugget many times throughout my life—in work situations, client meetings, walking into a room where I knew no one. And it has served me well.

SEVENTEEN

ACCEPTING HELP DOES NOT MEAN YOU'RE WEAK (BUT KEEP DOING IT YOUR WAY)

Isn't it odd the way that once we become parents, we suddenly notice how everyone around us, including the neighbor's dog, seems to be better at the whole parenting thing than we are? I'm not even kidding. When my eldest daughter was around two years old, that neighbor's dog had a litter of puppies. Duchess was her name. She loved to lie on her owner's back deck with her head held high while her well-behaved litter snuggled up against her. And may I add, contentedly. Eyes closed, I could see their smiling little muzzles. Meanwhile, my kid was throwing a tantrum because it was time to come in for her nap. Momma dog had seven puppies under control. I was barely managing my one. Duchess felt superior, and who could blame her? (Although I may have hated her. Just a little.)

My point? In case you think it's just you, nothing makes you feel more incompetent at life than your own kids. Clarification: I am not blaming your kids for the way you feel. I don't even know your kids. And I'm not blaming my kids for the amount of sucking I do at life either. And I *do* know my kids. (On most days.) There's just something about parenting that strips us of our own self-confidence—which, when you put it down on paper as I just have, sounds ridiculous, right? Seriously, how could being a parent bring out all of our most ugly traits and put them on center stage of our everyday lives? Could it be because we feel *uncaring* when our kids want us to sit down and watch *SpongeBob SquarePants* with them and we suddenly get the urge to clean out the garage? Or maybe it's because we feel *mean* every time we say no to one more cookie, or *selfish* when we want three minutes by ourselves so that we can pull down our pants and pee without having to answer a stream of questions that suddenly make us reexamine our own anatomy. *(Why do you have hair there, Mommy?)*

These are just a few theories I've developed over the years—and trust me, I've had many years to think about this. At the same time, though, I think it's only fair to say that parenting also helps us grow and come into ourselves as individuals. The role of parent teaches us patience while at the same time forcing us to instill rules and boundaries—the very things that children need to feel safe and loved (ironically). I am not making this shit up. Before I continue on *this* tangent, let's take a little detour, shall we?

Once upon a long time ago (translation: when I was a kid), parents' focus and concern were on their children's *behavior*. A kid acted up, and she was reprimanded for it, whether with a spanking (which is practically illegal today), or by being sent to her room, or by having to hear those horrible words: "there will be no TV for you until you're thirty-seven years old." (Which, in my case, was fine, because I already had plans to move out on my own the day after my fourth birthday.) Today's parenting approach has switched gears to put emphasis on children's *feelings*. While this is important, I'm going to go ahead and say that it's probably not as important as how they *behave*.

Confession: the following has entered my mind more than once when my kids were misbehaving: "If you want to *feel* good, then stop *behaving* like an asshole."

Of course, I never actually said that out loud, because *that* would be bad parenting, and child services would be knocking on my door faster than I could say "awwwww, did Mommy hurt your *feelings*?" #sarcasm

So, part of your own opinion about your own inadequacies as a parent stems from your fear of being judged by society, by your parents, by your friends, and even by the neighbor's damn dog. The truth is that there is no right or wrong way to parent. Almost. I say almost because as I write this, I'm thinking about a woman I once knew.

I feel another tangent coming on . . .

I was in my mid-twenties and had quasi-bonded with another woman because she, too, was a single mom. Our kids went to the same elementary school, and I first noticed her after I fell in love with her British accent. She was new to the country, I soon learned, and alone with her six-year-old son. Also, it was the month of December. As soon as I found out that she had nobody to spend the holidays with, I did what any sane person would do: I invited her to spend Christmas Eve with my two girls, my mother, and me.

For the sake of respecting other people's privacy, we'll call this woman Rebecca and her son . . . hmm, what would be a good name for her son? Oh, I know! *Satan.* Rebecca was of the thinking (new thinking, even for back then) that a child's *feelings* are the most important thing in the world. Even more important than the price of rice in China on market day. (I have no idea why I just said that.)

So, it's Christmas Eve day, and my mom comes over to cook a turkey and all the fixings while I clean my apartment and get my girls ready because "we're having company." Preparing for the evening's celebration took the entire day, because "special occasion" and "new friends" and whatever. I guess back then I wanted to make a big deal out of December 24.

Then, at three-thirty in the afternoon we hear it: *ding dong*. Not the clock, but the doorbell. Although it may as well have been a clock, because our guests were precisely one hour early. "No worries," I thought. "It's four-thirty somewhere." And the four of us—my two girls, Mom, and I—practically skipped to the door to greet our guests with enthusiasm. Gracious and smiling, Rebecca delicately stepped over the threshold and into my apartment, while Satan whipped in like the Tasmanian devil—unaware at that precise moment that the festivities (and intentions) for the evening had suddenly taken a new direction. Think whirlwind and a lot of swearing.

By the time Rebecca and Satan (finally) left, there were broken dishes on the kitchen floor, peas had rolled into tiny crevices where I'm certain some are still hiding in fear all these years later, and many of my girls' dolls were left headless and horrified. And my living room? OMGness. Let me tell you about my living room. Alas, I'm getting ahead of myself. Let me go back, regardless of how hard this memory is on my sense of wanting to develop friendships with quasi-strangers.

My most vivid memory of that evening was after supper when we were all sitting in—you guessed it—my living room. If you can imagine for a second a group of people relaxing on Christmas Eve after the blessed enjoyment of a meal together. All randomly seated on the L-shaped couch and badly matching accent chairs, chatting. Perhaps asking questions with personal interest, sharing stories about the previous week, or elaborating on opinions about the latest celebrity gossip. Christmas music softly playing in the background.

Sounds delightful, but there was none of that. My girls were crying because their toys were broken. My mother sat wide-eyed as she politely struggled to stifle a scream—the kind of scream you hear in a mental institution. Rebecca was pitifully cooing to Satan, "Please sit still. Come see Mommy . . ." Meanwhile, Satan had jumped from my couch into my curtains, grabbing the fabric à la Tarzan on his way down. Me? I was paralyzed as I watched my entire living room get destroyed. It happened very quickly and yet very slowly. Quick in time. Slow in motion. Little Satan had ruined the entire celebration from the moment he came spinning into my home. Rebecca was the type of parent who focused on her ~~savage's~~ child's *feelings*.

Okay, I need to stop right here. As I write this, I'm actually reliving the horror of that day. Slightly hyperventilating. Yet on the other side of the parenting pendulum, you wouldn't want to tie your kid to a tree and leave them there while you binge-watch reruns of *Friends* either. **cough**

(By the way, I ran into Rebecca about a decade later, when Satan was in high school, and I'm happy to report that at the time, he was an honor student and not a juvenile delinquent, as I'd predicted he'd turn out to be.)

My point? Regardless of how incompetent you feel as a parent, you *are* doing your best. I know this because I've been there, and as our kids are growing and developing into humans, so are we as parents, as individuals—as super-women. In fact, parenting actually helps us in our development. Or at least it can, if we let it. Parenting brings us on a journey of phases, beginning with the Ugly.

During the Ugly phase, not only do you feel inadequate in your parenting abilities but things start to come out of your mouth that you never thought you'd say in a million lifetimes. *(Stop wiping your snots on my leg.)* Before I had children, I was chill and carefree, *I swear.* And then I became a mother, and suddenly it was like I had to instill all these rules or the world, including my house and sanity, would crack and split into a thousand fragments. This change in personality (and language) marks the beginning of the loss of self-confidence. "Who am I?" you ask your mirrored reflection. And of course, your mirrored reflection doesn't respond with an answer as Mary Poppins's reflection does, because *you're not Mary freaking Poppins.* And so you find yourself in the middle of a muddled chaos of questions and self-doubt. I call this muddle the Bad.

This phase is when you completely—and I do mean *completely*—lose your sense of who you are. And with that, you also lose your confidence. I'm thinking that this is because with your new parenting responsibilities comes the opening of the door to advice—wanted and unwanted—from everyone you come into contact with. It's as though you're wearing a T-shirt that reads, "I have children and they ate my common sense. All of it. Please remind me how to be a human."

And for a while, you listen to your parents' advice on discipline. You sit quietly as your neighbor's dentist tells you about the importance of maintaining a strict bedtime routine. You even pay attention to what the older ladies at the grocery store have to say about teething and its many surprise symptoms, such as diarrhea, rashes, and sleepless nights. And don't even get me started on the kids' symptoms.

Since becoming a mother, I've received more advice on how to parent than on any other topic. And it seems that the more people have told me how I should (or shouldn't) mother, the more I felt like I wasn't managing well at all, from "don't let her play with sticks, she'll poke out her eyes" to "he should just do what he's told, without you having to negotiate with him." This is because when everyone has an opinion on you, your kids, and your parenting, you begin to question yourself on *everything*.

Is seven o'clock too early to put them to bed?

Should I make her eat all her supper, or is saying "two more bites" going to lead her into a career of serial killer?

How much computer time is too much before his brain turns into a melted mess of gooey binaries? (Not sure what a binary is? Good. You're my kind of people.)

This phase can go on for years. Then one morning, you wake up and realize that everyone telling you how to parent is making you question your own sense of self. You're afraid to make a breakfast decision. You're unsure about the way you stack your dishes in the dishwasher. You even question your choice of vegetables with supper. Hmm, broccoli or peas? The truth is, it doesn't matter. *They're both vegetables, and they're both green.*

This is when you decide that all the interference has to stop, taking you into the third phase of parenting: the Good. You're polite about it, of course. You still listen (or rather, you let everyone talk), but you begin to pay attention to how what they're saying resonates with your own principles and values. You begin to listen to the way that YOU *feel.* And then you remember that no one knows your kid better than you.

"Play with sticks? Of course you can play with sticks," you say as you recognize that sticks are a great way to get your kids to play outside with their own imagination instead of sitting in the house with their tablet. (And besides, has anyone ever really poked her eyes out because she was playing with sticks? I'm pretty sure the answer to that is *no.*)

"How about if you wear your Spider-Man pajamas as soon as you get home from school," you rationalize as you think to yourself, *Hmm . . . I wonder if this means he'll want to go to bed early—am I on to something here?*

All in all, becoming a parent is a process of noticing a change in the things that come out of your mouth, losing a bit of your confidence, and realizing that you've perhaps misplaced some pieces of yourself. And just as you start to come to terms with all of this, you begin to use your own wings and learn to accept that sometimes you'll even make mistakes. And guess what? That's okay. After all, our parents made mistakes, and we turned out okay. (Except for you, Ted Bundy. You did *not* turn out okay.)

Meanwhile, the people around you will continue to offer advice. And the people who love you will continue to offer their support. Accept it. Accept it all. Take the advice that you *feel* in your heart of hearts is good advice *for you.* Accept the offers to babysit while you take a night course or a dance class. Perhaps you can even offer to have another single mother's kids over for a playdate and give *her* a well-deserved break.

Not only do we all need time for ourselves but letting other people in our kids' lives is also healthy for them. Meanwhile, remain mindful of what's right for you and your kids. Don't let anyone take away your power. You're the mom. Own it.

A CHAT WITH
MARLENE
QUEBEC, CANADA

Thoughts on dating as a single mom

WHEN IT COMES TO DATING, we all have our stories. And if we put them all together in a laundry bag, you could bet that we'd have several years' worth of stories to share and laugh over. Let's face it: we would probably run out of wine before we ran out of stories. And while many of our stories may make us want to scream from the rooftops ("What was I thinking?!"), our dating experiences also provide us with an opportunity to learn something about ourselves. Usually something important.

Enter Marlene, a single mother of four now-grown children, and an advocate for online dating. And by advocate, I don't mean like the flawless actors that we see on TV commercials, fake bragging about how they found true love on the latest, trendiest online dating site.

While it wasn't easy, Marlene actually did find true love online. Marlene got to go through the online dating merry-go-round twice. The first time was after her first divorce. She was thirty years old, and because she was married at a young age, she'd never really gotten to experience the dating scene prior to her first marriage. With three children in tow at the time, her first reaction was relief.

"I remember feeling like a great weight had finally been lifted off my shoulders," says Marlene as she recalls her life after her first marriage ended.

You may recognize this as the first symptom associated with leaving an unhappy relationship. This is a good indication that you've made the right decision. It means that no matter how hard you know life is going to be as a single mother, you've just broken free from some of the burden that comes with living in an unhappy relationship.

Although never really a party girl, Marlene's initial reaction to her newfound freedom was to celebrate. A lot. Not looking for anything serious at that time, she even dyed her hair blonde because, according to the media, "blondes have more fun." A natural brunette, Marlene now knows that this is false advertising. Although Marlene's headspace at the time wasn't to meet "the one," she did meet the man who would become her second husband less than a year later.

"When I separated from my second husband, everything—my situation, even myself—was totally different. I was now thirty-seven years old, had four kids, and felt 'this big,'" she explains while holding up two fingers less than an inch apart to describe her sense of self-worth. Trying not only to find her place in the world but also to feel better about herself, Marlene rediscovered her passion for dancing and joined a ballroom dance group.

"This helped me a lot," she says of the support she gained through this social activity.

Not ready to get involved with anyone, and to help avoid the confusion between needing sex and needing someone in her life, Marlene developed friendships for different situations. She had friends for movies, friends for intimacy, and friends for simply hanging out. "It wasn't easy to meet people," she admits. "Everywhere I went, people were either too young or too old. It seemed there was no one in my age group or in my situation."

Marlene recalls one evening in particular when she was out with a group of other singles. "We were sitting at a table, and a man I didn't know put his hand on the back of my chair. This was his way of showing everyone that he was making claims on me," she recalls. "During the conversation, another woman asked about my situation. As I'm telling her that I've been married twice, divorced twice, have four kids and start reciting their ages, I noticed my girlfriend sitting on the other side of the table start laughing like crazy. Even though I wasn't saying anything funny, I knew why she was laughing, because I could feel the man whose hand was on my chair start to move away from me."

Admittedly, Marlene didn't have many real boyfriends—men she could say were "in her life"—during the first years after her second divorce. But she did go out on several dates.

"Most of the men I dated, I met through dating sites," she admits. "And dating at that time was always tricky because I had full custody of my kids."

Eventually, Marlene did bring a certain man home and introduced him to her daughters as her boyfriend. It was this man, a man we'll call Jeffery, who gave her the ah-ha moment that would change the way she viewed men, relationships, and even herself.

"Jeffery was a turning point in my life. He actually lived with me for a while, and one morning I just woke up and thought, 'Oh my God, I'm making the same mistake *again*!'"

This is when Marlene realized that she was repeatedly attracting the same kind of man. Comparing her first husband with her second husband and just about every man in between, including Jeffery, she suddenly saw the pattern.

"I don't remember what it was exactly that made me realize it, but it wasn't until I asked Jeffery to leave and was gathering all of his belongings that I noticed the empty bottles hidden at the back of my closet."

This realization dawned on Marlene like a falling house. Suddenly every man she had ever been with—from the short and blond to the tall and dark—were the same person. Marlene realized at that point that the type of men she was attracting were all looking for a mother. Someone to take care of things. And by things, I mean everything. All the things.

"That's when I made the decision that I deserved better," she says with conviction.

Once she realized this, it was easier for her to notice when the same "type" of man was entering into her life. It was also easier for her to not waste time on yet another life lesson.

Today, Marlene is happily involved with a *real* life partner—someone she loves and respects. And in case you're wondering, she met him through a dating site.

"My current boyfriend is the first man that I actually feel like we're a team together. We complete each other in a true sense. Whether we're cooking, cleaning, watching a movie, doing nothing, doing something—everything is fun because it's the two of us doing it together. I realize now that before, even when I was with someone, I was always missing that sense of togetherness."

To be alone—by yourself, with your children—is difficult. But to be alone, in a relationship with someone—that's real loneliness. Marlene knows now that love is not about surrendering to its pain but about rising to your best. And the person you choose (yes, you always have a choice in this) should foster your best, not inhibit it. Another superwoman gets her cape!

EIGHTEEN

OF COURSE, THIS BOOK WOULDN'T BE COMPLETE WITHOUT A CHAPTER ON THE LOVELY TASK OF RAISING TEENAGERS

YOU. YES, YOU. PERSON WHO is reading this right now. While I can't claim to know you personally, there is one thing that I know for sure. It's actually something that we have in common. And here it is: at one time, we both went through the very conflicting, if not volatile, experience of being a teenager. You see? We're practically best friends. And who knows? Maybe we even hung out for a while, because we all know that making friends when you're a teenager is relatively easy. Or, at least easier than making friends once you enter the even more conflicting, if not volatile, experience of trying to pass as an adult.

Regardless, I'm pretty sure you'll agree that the teenage years of a person's life are not the most glorious. In fact, they kinda suck. Let's face it: it's hard being a teenager. The experts blame hormones, but I believe it's deeper than that. It's several years of awkwardness and feeling self-conscious and wanting to be popular and feeling that you're not accepted and that you don't belong anywhere. I think I just described *every* life stage, but for some reason it's hardest during the teenage years. Perhaps because of the hormones. Okay, so maybe the experts are right after all.

Here's something else we can perhaps agree on: there's only one thing that's more difficult than being a teenager, and that is being the mother of a teenager. And yes, I'm speaking from experience here—my own and that of other single mothers with whom I've spoken. Just recently, I spoke at an event about the importance of remembering who you are and not defining yourself by your status. You know the one: the single mother status. During my talk I shared some of my experiences as a single mother. Later that day, a woman walked up to me and said that the hardest thing about single parenting is trying to navigate the mess of raising teenagers. And she's right. Teenagers *are* messy. They're old enough to cook yet seem unprepared to tackle the part where the kitchen needs cleaning up afterward. They're old enough to go out on their own on a Saturday night yet can't seem to comprehend common courtesies. Like letting you know that they're *still alive* after midnight.

While I'm not here to pretend to be the Grand Poobah of parenting, I have found that what helps (besides a well-stocked wine rack) is stepping into the time machine and remembering what it was like for you, the once-teenager now-turned-adult parent to a teenager. And to help, here are my top two reminders.

REMINDER 1: EYE-ROLLING BECOMES AN IMPORTANT LIFE SKILL

Everyone rolls her eyes. You did it when you were a teenager, and you're still doing it while your teenagers are doing it.

Except you may have noticed that there's a slight difference in the way that you used to roll your eyes (when you were a teenager) and the way you do it now. You know this from watching your kids. Just like you at their age, your teens do it with attitude. They put their entire socket muscles into it so that they can actually look back at their own spines—as though the rest of the world is completely and utterly ridiculous. (And there's no denying it—sometimes the rest of the world *actually is* completely and utterly ridiculous.)

Best way to react: Ignore. Don't respond. Don't feed the fire. Don't even make eye contact. Hold your breath and walk out of the room if you have to. And if it helps, rest assured that that very special talent your teens have of making you feel ludicrous will eventually fade away and reemerge in *their* kids. I call this *the real* cycle of life.

REMINDER 2: WHEN YOU'RE A TEENAGER, FEELING AWKWARD IS THE NEW NORM

This may be the very reason why there's so much eye-rolling going on. It serves as a cover-up for the way that teenagers really feel behind the attitude, which is often worn as a mask. While on the outside they're displaying the teenage act of defiance that we've come to love so much (yes, that was sarcasm), behind the mask sits a tiny person who feels like he simply doesn't fit in anywhere. Just the other day, I was out with my son, and we ran into a former colleague of mine. (Side note: my son doesn't usually like to be seen in public with me, but we were going out for dinner, and when there's food involved—well, you know how it is.) When I introduced my son, I noticed that he was very cordial. The words "it's nice to meet you" comfortably stumbled out of his mouth as he confidently extended his hand, meeting my former colleague halfway for a handshake. I watched with pride. Yet afterward, my son asked me if his awkwardness was obvious. I was shocked. To me, he looked cool as a cucumber. (Cool as a cucumber? What are we, the seventies?)

Best way to react: Praise. Tell them that they did great, that you weren't even aware that they felt awkward. Also, tell them—remind them—that everyone feels awkward at times and that the best way to push through is to just act like a human being, not an eye-rolling teenager. (Although you may not want to mention that last part out loud.)

BONUS LIFE HACK: HOW TO GET YOUR TEENAGERS
TO STOP SWEARING

I don't know about your household, but in my house, it happened overnight. One day my kids were all sweet and polite with dimples and no sign of hormones anywhere. The next day I was dealing with attitude and multiple trips to the store for pimple cream. The day after that, my teens had taken to swearing when I was in another room. They *thought* I couldn't hear them, but what they didn't realize was that as their mom, *I hear everything*. If your kids are on the brink of Tasmanian-teenage hell, you know what I'm talking about. It's just one of the many symptoms of being a parent, and it goes something like this:

Have kids. Develop bionic hearing.

It's also the reason why people all over the world refer to parents, especially single mothers, as "demi-gods." (So I've heard.) So how did I react when my teenagers started swearing behind my back? I ignored it. Why? Because many years ago, I learned another important life skill: picking my battles. At the time, my oldest daughter was going through the terrible twos and having a meltdown in aisle 4. She wanted Cocoa Puffs, and I had made the fatal mistake of saying no. Enter the wrath of a two-year-old. I still shiver in horror at the sight of a box of Cocoa Puffs.

Then when that same toddler morphed overnight into a teenager on the verge of developing bad language habits, I learned not to cringe, neither internally nor externally, and to hold my face in place when walking into a room after profanities had been flung about with F-bombs still sticking to the walls like a spaghetti dinner gone wrong. This type of composure takes practice.

Also, I may have unconsciously programmed my brain to automatically bleep out all words that begin with the letters *b, f,* and *sh.* And let's not forget that I, too, was a teenager at their age. Just the fact that they were using such words "behind my back" meant that there was still hope. It made me feel like maybe—just maybe—I still had some clout. If nothing, I'm hopeful.

One of the saddest aspects of being a parent to sweet children is that they eventually do morph into teenagers. That's when things get tricky. Those same sweet children start coming home with new ideas, opinions . . . words. Suddenly, snuggling under a blanket and watching a Disney movie together isn't "their thing." They want to watch YouTubers pull practical jokes on their dogs, and they want to do it by themselves—in their room with the door closed. (This is a sign that they do not want to be bothered. But feel free to come get them when FOOD.)

And of course, they will test us. That's what teens do, and that's why we have them—so that we can excel at passing these tests. It's our rite of passage into adulthood. Don't say you heard it from me, but teenagers are our very own personal incentive for growing up. But all is well. I have my black belt in parenting, and I'm about to share a secret with you. It's a method I developed years ago when my teens had just crossed the threshold into who-are-you-and-what-have-you-done-with-my-angels. It's a proven two-step process for getting your teens to stop using those *b* and *f* and *sh* words.

The way I see it, swear words are a healthy part of a balanced vocabulary. They help us cope with frustrating situations, and they alleviate stress. I haven't actually found scientific proof of this yet, except that it's a tested theory.

Tested in my own life situations. And since we all want our teens to grow into healthy adults, the secret is not to eliminate swear words but to replace them.

Here's how this two-step process works:

Step 1. Introduce new words.
Step 2. Make said new words sound badass.

I know what you're thinking: *It sounds too simple. This can't possibly work.* Trust me. It does. And to help get you started, here's a list of suggested replacement words. (Let's see if you can figure out the original phrases.)

What the what?
Cheese 'n' rice!
Stop talking junk!

You can also use one word to replace all swear words. Here are some examples using the word *fish*:

Fish off!*
Go fish yourself!*
Fish!*
Bullfish!*
Shut the fish up!*

*Use of the exclamation mark is optional but highly recommended. It's the sprinkled-on spice of badass I mentioned earlier.

As a mother, you can imagine how proud I am when I'm reading quietly on the living room couch, or folding towels in the laundry room, and I hear my teens yelling "go fish yourself!" or "get out of my fishen' room!"

It really is quite endearing. And just another small win on the parenting front line.

In conclusion, parenting teens is not easy. It's not easy

today, it wasn't easy for our parents, and it wasn't easy during the King Tut era. But if you can go into your teenager's psyche and master these simple raising-teenager life hacks, you may even be able to cut down on your wine consumption. Except why would you want to do that? Wine is cheaper than therapy.

NINETEEN

YOU ARE A FAMILY

CONFESSION: WRITING THIS CHAPTER WAS a struggle. The words kept coming out, and yet my brain wasn't sure about what I was trying to say. I wasn't even sure how to unravel the tangled confusion of my thoughts on this subject. I'm guessing that living with regret is never easy. People talk about how you can't go back and fix things. This is true. What's also true—and what we often don't give ourselves permission to acknowledge—is that we always do the best we can at the time. Regrets come "after"—once we're a little smarter, a little wiser, a little more skilled in the ways of life. Regrets are the child of hindsight. They're born of new perspectives and understandings.

This realization came to me earlier this morning as I was sitting in my living room, writing in my headbook. (Perhaps you call yours a journal.) That's when the act of swirling words and emotions on the page made me realize that regret is the afterthought of experience and that this is actually an important chapter. It was as though the rising sun peeking through the crooked slit in the blinds put a spotlight on my own understanding of regret, yearning, family, and trust. And then when I got up to fix the blinds (not because I'm neurotic but because I needed some space to absorb the moment), I realized that by "trust," I actually mean the deep, jagged edges of untrust.

Allow me to explain what that means. Untrust. It's like living with a condition. If you live with it, you know exactly what I'm talking about. If you don't, consider yourself lucky. That's not sarcasm. I truly and simply mean *consider yourself lucky*. Living with the hollow feeling of untrust is terrible. Heavier than feelings of insecurity, untrust is a dark shadow that casts a powerful spell on your core as it settles there for you to battle with every single day. In essence, you're battling with yourself. And much like a childhood teddy bear that's filthy from time, you want to rid yourself of it—you try to outgrow it—and in your attempts you realize that you don't even know how, that this sense of untrust has become a part of who you are. It's emotionally paralyzing and does bad things to your self-esteem. A tangled ball of emotional twine, it sits like a clump of indigestible food in your chest. Untrust. I wouldn't wish it on anyone.

I believe that untrust is born from situations that cause hurt and disappointment. It could be just one big blow at a vulnerable age or a series of sharp jabs that eventually break us into a thousand yearning pieces. Over time, feeling whole becomes our purpose. And for much of my life, feeling whole has been something that I strived to achieve. Except that I was going about it all wrong. I was looking for the answers on the outside. The best example I can give is that for most of my adult life, I so wanted a "life partner"—someone who would make me feel like I belonged. I wanted to love and be loved. I wanted to be "home" with someone I could feel 100 percent secure with. Someone I could love, trust, and admire. Over the years, I've been in relationships in which I felt loved and trusted, or trusted and admired, or admired and loved—but the triangle was never complete. I never felt all three for the same person at the same time. Ever. I knew something was missing. I saw the red flags; I just chose to ignore them. And now that I've reached "this age," I've also come to realize that ignoring the red flags is something I'm very good at. If there was a category in the Olympics for dodging red flags, I would hold gold.

I've also learned to recognize that part of what hindered me from finding what I so desperately wanted was my own self. The untrust made me raise a shield of discerning protection. It was conflicting for me, so I can only imagine how confusing it would be for someone else—someone who perhaps was trying to get close to me. Half of my heart desperately wanted to be the perfectly fitted piece of a couple. The other half of my heart was afraid of being disappointed. When you live with untrust, disappointment turns into disillusionment, and you eventually learn to avoid it at all costs. And so, to protect myself, I established my own personal creed, one void of any sense of anticipation. It goes something like this: *no expectations, no disappointments.*

Sounds great in theory, but it isn't. Without expectations, you're also left with no real standards. You accept the unacceptable, ignoring that you, like everyone else, are deserving of what you desire. For me, it was a sense of belonging. A sense of family.

Life becomes the glass window of a fancy store. From where you stand outside, you watch families with a mom and a dad and children. A family unit. The mutual support. The shared appreciation of joint creations. The parents, two poles leaning on each other—complementing their differences—as they beam with pride and observe both their children and their relationship grow. What's his is hers. What's hers is his. What's theirs is never questioned or taken for granted. They *know* how each day will end. Together.

On the outside of the window, you. Alone. A single pole held up by the tugging ropes of the many tasks and responsibilities surrounding you. You're always aware of the little minds and mouths that need constant feeding. Your children. You love them with every fiber of your being. Yet on many days, their incessant needs deplete you. Not to say that all is easy for two-parent families. But when you put the kids to bed at night and end each day by yourself, even your own thoughts can add to the load.

Regret.

My mistake for many years was to believe that my kids and I weren't enough. That we—just us—were not a real family. On the outside, I held it together. I was the sole pillar. On the inside, something was always missing. The foundation. Although I've never spoken about this to my kids, I'm certain they felt it too. Not because it was true, but because I felt it. I made it our reality.

As a single mom, you become *the everything.* The mom, the dad, the nurturer, the provider. There's no yin and yang in your parenting skills or family unit because it all comes from you. Whether you're the disciplinarian or more of the easygoing type, you learn to fake the ghost side of the missing parenting role as a way to balance things out. I'm not a psychologist, but as I write this, a question crosses my mind—is this not confusing for our kids? I'm imagining that in a family with a mom and a dad, the kids always know to whom to turn, depending on the situation. Let's say that in this imaginary scenario, Mom is the "You don't want to eat your peas? No worries. Let's play loud music and dance on the coffee table!" and Dad is the "Have you done your homework? No? Well then, you can't play outside until it's done!"

When you're solo parenting, one day you're the easygoing type, and the next day you're strict as hell. The question: wouldn't this make the kids wonder if Mom isn't a little psychotic? Where's the consistency? The stability of roles and behavior? At least when you have two parents, you can predict how your parents will react, because each parent fits neatly into his or her role. And that role is consistent with his or her personality. Consistency. That's the key.

Among the many single mothers with whom I've had the pleasure of speaking during the writing of this book, I noticed that untrust, although perhaps not worded as such, is a strong, underlying theme. The BFF bracelet of our sister-hood and status is strung together with this sense of untrust, making us feel that we need to do it all ourselves. Learned or not, this sense of solitary parenting is the foundational belief of our aloneness. The truth is that we—our children and ourselves—really are a family unit, with or without a partner. What makes a family? A sense of safeness. Traditions. Shared family values and principles. My biggest regret is that I didn't understand this when my kids were younger.

But then again, wasn't I doing the best I could at the time? Yes, I was. And yes, I still am. And yes, I always will. Tomorrow will always hold a better perspective. As for today, we bring the best that we are in this time.

A CHAT WITH
CINDY RENAUD
QUEBEC, CANADA

Thoughts on time and place

CINDY'S* BOYS WERE FIVE AND two and a half years old when she and her husband divorced. At the time, she was in her mid-thirties. Some would argue that this is the peak age to focus on one's career. But not in this case. For Cindy, her boys were her priority, and during that time, she turned down what she still considers a "job of a lifetime."

"My ex-husband and I worked very hard to maintain a collaborative arrangement after our divorce," Cindy explains, "which is why I turned down that opportunity. We certainly couldn't both be in our sons' lives if he was in Canada and I was in Europe."

The year was 1989 and the world a different place.

"It was a tough decision, but at the same time, I was optimistic. I believed that other opportunities would come up when the time was right. That's how I approached it."

At the time, Cindy worked in the IT industry, a thriving and growing field. If you can imagine, this is a time before

---

*Name has been changed at the individual's request.

the internet. Personal computers were just being introduced. And social media, not having been invented yet, was still a distraction for future generations.

"There were quite a lot of women in IT at the time, and I think that's because there was a skill shortage in this relatively new field," explains Cindy.

While genders definitely had their roles at the time, Cindy's path crossed both. With a degree in engineering, her goal was to become a building architect, which she later switched over to digital architecture. As we know today, IT is a predominantly male-oriented vocation.

As a mother, Cindy's upbringing encouraged her to be the primary caregiver. "I come from a very traditional background," she explains. "I couldn't imagine not being the principal nurturer of my babies. And my ex-husband, while he was a great daddy, he was a terrible mommy. His concept of diet, activity, and sleep—he just didn't have any major thinking going on about these things. He cared for our kids, of course, but he was more typical of his generation."

So, Cindy continued to work at a job that she enjoyed yet didn't find fulfilling. As well, she appreciated the fact that her immediate boss, also a woman, was very family-friendly and understood the demands of being a single mother. Juggling both a job and the role of single mother, Cindy's biggest challenge was time management.

"I made a lot of planning decisions based on my target structure," she explains. "For instance, I bought a house within fifteen walking minutes from my ex-husband's house. The house was also a five-minute drive to both my mother's house and my mother-in-law's. I wanted to make sure that I had a lot of backup and support for the kids."

While being financially independent was important to Cindy, she knew that making sure she had the help she needed would only benefit both herself and her boys. As I write this, I need to acknowledge Cindy for her insights. For many of us, myself included, asking for help is one of the most difficult things we can do. For some reason, we've conditioned ourselves to believe that we must do it all. At the end of the day, we're left exhausted and often frustrated, which doesn't benefit anyone.

When I asked what advice she had for other single mothers, Cindy had this to say: "I would tell any mother to cut herself some slack and take the mommy track for a while. When I became a single mom, I went back to a company that I had worked for before and knew well. I did not display any extreme ambition for the next seven or eight years because I was happy to stay at that company. It wasn't always perfect, and I knew I could do better elsewhere, but I also knew that that just wasn't possible for me at that time if I wanted to make my kids my priority, which I did.

"I valued my children and I valued making them the priority. I figured when they got to be a certain age and wouldn't need me as much, that would be my time to do more.

"The other point I want to make is that a career is not a straight ladder going up. Sometimes you move sideways. Sometimes you temporarily take a step down to be able to take a bigger step up in a couple of years, when your circumstances are ready for it. Think of your career as a long-term climb up a mountain. And with every mountain, there are peaks and valleys before you get to the top."

What I love about Cindy's story is that it demonstrates the ability to put things on hold to focus on what is in line with our values. It doesn't matter what society says. Sure, some women want and need it all. There's no shame in either path.

Today, Cindy is a recognized leader in her field. A woman of substance. And a woman of no regrets. She's made some very difficult decisions and sacrifices. And yes, she's the definition of a superwoman.

TWENTY

DEAR YOUNGER ME . . .

I DON'T WANT ANY TROUBLE from you. Come in, bring your thoughts and an open mind, and have a seat. Just don't touch anything.

So, you wanted a family. You craved for that solid foundation that you thought would come from feeling like you belong to a family unit—a real family with a mother, a father, children, and perhaps a dog, a cat, and a parrot. Here's the deal: it didn't happen, and it will never happen for you. Despite that, I've learned that everything happens for a reason. As I think back to the early days of single motherhood, I remember you with a dreaded sense of disappointment. You felt frustrated, and even overwhelmed a lot of the time. Fear was also a daily companion.

While much of what you felt was the result of decisions you made, I can share this: one day in the far distant future, you will long for the days when the kids were young and still yours. Meanwhile, you wonder if this is it. Well, it's not. There's so much more coming your way; you're just not ready yet. Your destiny is not ready yet, and neither is your purpose. If everything came easily to you, you'd settle into a life. You wouldn't strive for more. And there really is more for you. More for you to receive and more for you to give.

Speaking to you from eleven thousand years into the future, your children and even your status are gifts. You will grow up with your children, and your status as a single mother will show you your own strength—in fact, more than show: it will settle into you.

At some point you'll realize that you can't do it all, and guess what? That's okay. On some days you'll focus on yardwork and let the house go. On other days your mind will be on work and you'll end up burning dinner. In fact, you'll do that a lot. This is where you'll learn to laugh at yourself—also a gift. And know this: none of that can happen if you continue to be so damn hard on yourself. Being tired at the end of the day doesn't mean you're giving up. It simply means you're tired. Go to bed.

And let's talk about standards for a minute. Get some. You, like everyone else, *deserve* to be happy. I believe Charlie Chaplin expressed it best when he said, "Nothing is permanent in this wicked world, not even our troubles." This is one of my favorite expressions because it's a reminder that while nothing is ever perfect, this, too, will pass.

As the days turn into years, you'll learn to let go. You'll learn to be kind to yourself. You'll even learn to like you. And from where I stand, you truly are doing your best, even on the days that you feel your best isn't good enough. Of course, there are things I would have loved for you to do differently, but saying this from a wiser place on a day for which the calendar hasn't yet been printed isn't really fair to you, is it? (As I write this, I just want to reach into the past and hug you.)

Dearest younger me, savor the present and keep looking ahead. Enjoy those kids. Relish each moment. One day, when you reach your mid-fifties, you will get a tattoo. You will have the words "Right here, right now" permanently plastered across the inside of your forearm. Perhaps you feel the tingle of ink on your skin. I tell you this because I wish I could go back and imprint that motto onto your brain. It took me years to appreciate the moment and even to bring my thoughts back into the present when my mind starts lingering on things that can't be changed. There's a lot of power in the present. Try to stay there. Regardless of how panicked, scared, or frustrated you feel, the future will come in its due time. Don't rush it.

One question that you ask often is, Are we still today? And the answer, the best answer, will come from your eldest daughter when she's in her twenties.

"Mom, it's always today."

I WOULD LOVE TO CONNECT WITH YOU!

Please take a selfie with the book and
tag me on your fave social media platform
so that I can personally thank you!
You can find me at either
@Mona_Andrei or @MoxieDude.
Meanwhile, *virtual high fives!*

CPSIA information can be obtained
at www.ICGtesting.com
Printed in the USA
BVHW021956010321
601250BV00005B/95